CW00544891

THE MECCAN REBELLION

The MECCAN
REBELLION

The Story of Juhayman al-'Utaybi Revisited

Thomas Hegghammer
and
Stéphane Lacroix

AMAL PRESS
BRISTOL • ENGLAND

Published by Amal Press, PO Box 688, Bristol BS99 3ZR, England

http://www.amalpress.com
info@amalpress.com

A CIP catalogue record for this book is available from the British Library

Thomas Hegghammer and Stéphane Lacroix, "The Meccan Rebellion: The Story of Juhayman al-'Utaybi Revisited," previously published as "Rejectionist Islamism in Saudi Arabia: The Story of Juhayman al-'Utaybi Revisited," *International Journal of Middle East Studies* 39(1):103-122, (2007) Copyright © 2007 Cambridge University Press.

The authors thank Gilles Kepel, Bernard Haykel, Greg Gause, Brynjar Lia, Steffen Hertog, Nabil Mouline, and the anonymous IJMES referees for their comments on earlier drafts of this article.

Stéphane Lacroix, "Between Revolution and Apoliticism: Nasir al-Din al-Albani and his Impact on the Shaping of Contemporary Salafism," reprinted, with kind permission of the publisher (www.hurstpub.co.uk), from Roel Meijer (ed.), *Global Salafism: Islam's New Religious Movement* (London: Hurst & Co., 2009).

Editorial changes have been made to both articles with permission of authors.

ISBN 978-0-95-5235993 cloth

Text design: Ian Abdallateef Whiteman /CWDM

Printed and bound in India by Replika Press Pvt. Ltd.

CONTENTS

INTRODUCTION

IN THE EARLY morning of 20 November 1979, a group of armed, rugged men appeared in the courtyard of the Grand Mosque in Mecca. Firing guns into the air, they walked briskly toward the Ka'ba, the black cube in whose direction all the world's Muslims pray. The rebels reached the old imam who had been leading the morning prayer and pushed him aside, brandishing a dagger. A heavily bearded man, who appeared to be their leader, grabbed the microphone and barked instructions to his companions who were scattered across the compound. They quickly closed all the gates and took up firing positions in the minarets and other strategic locations. The holiest site in Islam had been captured by rebels and tens of thousands of worshipers were trapped inside.

Thus began the Meccan rebellion, one of the most spectacular and tragic events to befall the Kingdom of Saudi Arabia, if not the whole Muslim world, in the twentieth century. For two full weeks the Grand Mosque compound remained under siege by Saudi security forces frantically trying to wrest control of the mosque from the unidentified rebels. By the time order was restored on 4 December 1979, hundreds of people were dead. Never before or since has so much blood been shed in this most sacred place of worship.

The scenario that unfolded in Mecca in late November 1979 was so bizarre and unexpected that no one, at the time, understood what was going on. Who would bring weapons into the Grand Mosque? Who would use them to hold peaceful worshipers hostage? Who would want bloodshed around the Ka'ba? To make matters worse, Saudi authorities quickly and completely restricted access to information about the developments in Mecca. Local and international phone lines were cut and roads were blocked off. While the hostages and security forces gradually came to realize what was happening, outsiders were left completely in the dark.

Soon, a flurry of rumors and conspiracy theories spread across Saudi Arabia and the world. Soviet media reported that the incident was part of a working-class uprising in the Hijaz region. The New York Times suggested that the attack was the work of Shia Muslims, inspired by the Iranian revolution. The Iranian media responded by calling the Meccan incident a US-orchestrated plot, prompting angry demonstrators in Pakistan to set the American embassy on fire and kill a US embassy employee. Many of these blatantly erroneous theories lingered for years and may in fact still be heard in some circles.

In the weeks following the end of the siege, the veil on the incident was partly lifted as the perpetrators were officially identified, briefly paraded on Saudi TV, and eventually executed. It turned out that the rebels were Sunni Islamists who subscribed to Salafi doctrines, mostly from Saudi Arabia, led by a Saudi tribesman named Juhayman al-'Utaybi. During the siege, Juhayman proclaimed that one of his companions, a certain Muhammad al-Qahtani, was the Mahdi—a messianic figure in Islam—and that they had come to consecrate him as such. The timing was ostensibly linked to the turn of the century (of the Islamic calendar). However, beyond a few cursory biographical details about the perpetrators and brief descriptions of the event, very little information emerged. Juhayman and his comrades were swiftly executed in January 1980, after which the veil of secrecy again fell on the Meccan rebellion. No official public inquiry was ever held, and independent journalists or scholars were never allowed to investigate the incident. Saudi authorities were generally tight-lipped about internal security issues, largely because this incident was so shocking and embarrassing for the government.

Over the next decades, a few writers tried to revisit the Meccan rebellion, but in the absence of reliable primary sources, no one was able to fully answer the most pressing question, namely, who were the rebels and what did they want? A widespread assumption was that the rebels represented a Saudi version of the revolutionary Islamist movements that had troubled Egypt and Syria around the same time. The Meccan rebels, it was often argued, proved the existence of a large domestic Islamist movement bent on toppling the House of Saud. Few, however, were able to explain why the rebels had chosen to attack, of all targets, the Grand Mosque in Mecca. Moreover, the details of the siege itself remained the subject of extensive speculation: how many people ultimately died? Were French special forces involved? Did they use chemical weapons to kill the rebels?

It was not until 2003 that we began to learn what had really happened. That year, Nasir al-Huzaymi, a former associate of the Meccan rebels, wrote a series of articles in the Saudi newspaper *al-Riyadh* about his experience as a member of Juhayman's group. For the first time in twenty-four years, we had an insider account. Al-Huzaymi had been active in the organization between 1976 and 1978, but left a year before the Meccan operation. He was caught in the police roundup after the event and spent eight years in prison, where he learned more about the siege itself from imprisoned rebels who had participated. Al-Huzaymi subsequently renounced his Islamist convictions and began working as a journalist.

Around the same time, Saudi authorities began to allow

more foreign academics and journalists to enter the country and conduct independent fieldwork. We were thus able to make contact with al-Huzaymi and begin researching the Meccan rebellion from inside the Kingdom. In 2007 we published our findings in an article in the *International Journal of Middle East Studies (IJMES)*. This book presents a revised and expanded version of this article.

Our main finding was that the Meccan rebellion was the work of an apocalyptic, charismatic sect with a very peculiar ideology. Its leaders genuinely believed that Muhammad al-Qahtani was the Mahdi, and that by consecrating him in Mecca on the turn of the hijri century, they would precipitate the end of the world and the series of associated events promised in the Islamic eschatological tradition. Juhayman and his closest comrades developed these beliefs during the two years before the takeover, when they lived in isolation in the desert.

We also show that the rebels represented an offshoot of a less radical, but previously unknown organization called al-Jama'a al-Salafiyya al-Muhtasiba (JSM), which had operated openly in Medina from the late 1960s onward. The JSM, we argue, represented a previously understudied subcurrent of Saudi Islamism, which we termed "rejectionist Islamism," in reference to its active rejection of the state and its institutions. While the JSM and the Meccan rebels died out in Saudi Arabia in the early 1980s, other parts of the rejectionist movement lived on.

The JSM was greatly inspired by the ideas of a shaykh named Muhammad Nasir al-Din al-Albani (1914–99). Because al-Albani remains relatively unknown outside Salafi circles, and because exploring his background, ideas and positions is important for understanding JSM, we added a second chapter to the book based on an article by Stéphane Lacroix.

Born in Syria, the son of an Albanian clockmaker, al-Albani was a complete outsider to the world of Salafism, which, in his time, remained largely identified with a few scholarly families

from the central Arabian region of Najd—families that con-
stituted the Saudi religious establishment. After adopting the
key principles of Salafism—to such an extent that he was invited to teach at the Islamic University of Medina in the early
1960s—he sparked a significant controversy by pointing out
what he considered to be a fundamental contradiction of Saudi
Salafis: they claimed to be faithful to the pious predecessors (*al-
salaf al-salih*), but they were de facto followers of the Hanbali
school of law. Al-Albani, in contrast, advocated the rejection
of all established schools, and sole reliance on the Qur'an and,
even more so, the hadith, to which he gave considerable importance. In other terms, al-Albani told the established Salafi
shaykhs that he was truer to the essence of Salafism than they
were. This position earned him recognition in certain circles,
especially among individuals from groups excluded from
Saudi social and religious hierarchies. Many of the members of
the JSM belonged to these excluded groups.

Al-Albani also rejected political activism, which he
considered damaging to the essence of preaching (*da'wa*). The
phrase "the good policy is to abandon politics" remains, until
today, his most quoted in Salafi circles. The JSM thus emerged
as a community fundamentally distrustful of politics, and
extremely critical of groups such as the Muslim Brotherhood.
This, we believe, sheds crucial light on the group's open
adoption of messianism from 1978 onward. While, for reasons
explained in the book, the JSM found itself increasingly in
conflict with the Saudi state, its refusal to embrace opposition
activism (and, more specifically, to excommunicate the Saudi
rulers) left it with only one option: waiting for a divine
intervention to save it from the predicament in which it found
itself. This intervention, JSM leaders believed, had come
in the form of Muhammad al-Qahtani, the proclaimed Mahdi.

An important disclaimer is needed here: our focus on al-
Albani is not meant to place any intellectual responsibility

on him for the Meccan rebellion. On the contrary, the vast majority of al-Albani's disciples have remained quietists, and have, in some cases, taken extremely pro-regime stances. In that sense, the JSM's radicalization is the exception that confirms the rule. Still, Juhayman's group offers a good illustration of the limits of the logic of apolitical rupture that the movement was advocating.

Since the scope of our research was limited to tracing the historical and ideological background of the perpetrators of the Meccan rebellion, we deliberately did not go into great detail about the siege itself. For a detailed and reliable account of the drama that unfolded in late November 1979, we refer the reader to Yaroslav Trofimov's book *The Siege of Mecca: The Forgotten Uprising in Islam's Holiest Shrine and the Birth of al-Qaida* (Doubleday, 2007). Trofimov's book is also based on extensive fieldwork in Saudi Arabia and stands as the definitive account of the siege. His interpretation of the ideological legacy of the Meccan rebels differs somewhat from ours, but his account complements our story very well.

Another important and relevant work that appeared after our *IJMES* article is Jean-Pierre Filiu's book, *Apocalypse in Islam* (University of California Press, 2011). Filiu reviews the history of apocalyptic thought and activism in Islam, of which the Meccan rebels are an important manifestation. Interestingly, Filiu documents a renaissance of popular apocalyptic writing across the Muslim world since the mid-1990s. In the Sunni world, this interest remains an intellectual phenomenon. In the world of Shiism, on the other hand, it has inspired political activism, notably in post-invasion Iraq, where the militant groups Jund al-Sama' and Ansar al-Mahdi were active in the mid- and late-2000s.

This prompts the question: Could the Meccan incident happen again? On the one hand, there is an inherent tension between messianism and activism, in the sense that those who believe in destiny may have few incentives to try to change it. On the other hand, fringe zealotry is notoriously difficult to predict. It would be imprudent to assume that apocalyptic activists will not emerge again. At the very least, future generations have reason to remain vigilant at the next turn of the hijri century, on 26 November 2076.

Thomas Hegghammer and Stéphane Lacroix
OSLO AND CAIRO, APRIL 2011

The MECCAN REBELLION

The Story of Juhayman al-'Utaybi Revisited

Thomas Hegghammer and Stéphane Lacroix

T HE STORMING OF the Grand Mosque in Mecca by Juhayman al-'Utaybi and his fellow rebels in November 1979 represents one of the most spectacular events in the modern history of Saudi Arabia. Yet it is one of the least understood. Even decades after the event, many important questions remain unanswered. Who were the rebels, and what did they want? Why and how did Juhayman's group come into existence?[1] What happened with the rebels and their ideas after the Mecca events? This chapter seeks to shed light on the story and legacy of Juhayman al-'Utaybi with new information gathered from extensive fieldwork in Saudi Arabia and elsewhere.

Whereas the details of the Mecca operation are relatively well known, the origin of the rebel group is shrouded in mystery.[2] The existing literature on Juhayman's movement is both sparse and contradictory. The interested student will find few in-depth studies of it in English.[3] The Arabic-language literature on Juhayman is somewhat more extensive and has certainly been underexploited by Western academics, but many works suffer from inaccuracies and political bias.[4] A key problem has been the absence of good primary sources, which has made it virtually impossible for historians to trace the origin and history of Juhayman's movement in any significant detail. This changed in 2003, when Nasir al-Huzaymi, a former associate of Juhayman al-'Utaybi, lifted the veil on his past and wrote a series of articles in the Saudi press about his experience as a member of Juhayman's group.[5] Al-Huzaymi had been active in the organization between 1976 and 1978 but left a year before the Mecca operation. He was caught in the police roundup after the event and spent eight years in prison. Al-Huzaymi has renounced his former Islamist convictions and now works as a journalist for the Saudi newspaper *al-Riyadh*.

Al-Huzaymi is one of several former Islamist radicals in Saudi Arabia who, from the late 1990s onward, began speaking publicly about his experiences as an activist.[6] Although their emergence at this particular point in time was facilitated by the process of limited liberalization initiated by Crown Prince 'Abdallah in 1999 and to some extent exploited by authorities as a counterbalance to conservative Islamist forces, it was by no means orchestrated by the state. These repentants emerged gradually in independent communities and began speaking out before 9/11 or the 2003 terrorist campaign in Saudi Arabia. There are strong reasons to take al-Huzaymi's testimony seriously. His account is descriptive, unflattering toward the authorities, and above all, consistent with other key historical sources.

The current chapter is based on a detailed reading of the available English- and Arabic-language literature about Juhayman, as well as on extensive fieldwork. During a series of research visits to Saudi Arabia and Kuwait, the authors of this book interviewed Nasir al-Huzaymi and several other former Saudi Islamists with in-depth knowledge of the Juhayman movement and phenomenon. By means of a generous intermediary, we obtained the testimony of a senior Medina-based cleric who was very close to Juhayman's group in the 1970s and attended the Grand Mosque during the 1979 siege. We traced the anonymous authors of the main Arabic books about Juhayman al-'Utaybi published in the early 1980s to identify and assess their primary sources.[7] We also spoke to journalists who covered the Juhayman story in the Mecca area in 1979. During this two-year research process, we were able to collect the accounts of several individuals, in addition to Nasir al-Huzaymi, who were either part of Juhayman's group or eyewitnesses to key events in the group's history.

This chapter is divided into three parts. The first and most voluminous part is devoted to the history of Juhayman's movement leading up to the storming of the Grand Mosque in 1979. In the second part, we reflect on the nature of this movement and evaluate existing theories and interpretations of the phenomenon. Finally, we examine the ideological legacy of Juhayman al-'Utaybi and his influence on subsequent radical movements in Saudi Arabia up to the present day. The chapter presents two central arguments. First, our research shows that the group that stormed the Grand Mosque in 1979 was a radicalized faction of a much broader pietistic organization set up in Medina in the mid-1960s under the name of al-Jama'a al-Salafiyya al-Muhtasiba (JSM), that is, the Salafi[8] Group that Commands Right and Forbids Wrong. The second main argument is that the JSM and its radical offshoot, Juhayman's Ikhwan (Brotherhood), were among the first manifestations of a particular type of Saudi Islamism that outlived Juhayman and has played an important yet subtle role in the shaping of the country's political landscape until today. It is characterized by a strong focus on ritual practices, a declared disdain for politics, and yet an active rejection of the state and its institutions.⁹ This so-called "rejectionist Islamism" is intellectually and organizationally separate from the other and more visible forms of Saudi Islamist opposition such as the so-called "awakening" (al-Sahwa) movement or the Bin Ladin style jihadists.¹⁰

Opposition and Islamism in Saudi Arabia before 1979

There have been relatively few cases of violent opposition to the rule of the Al Sa'ud since the foundation of the third Saudi state by 'Abd al-'Aziz b. Sa'ud in 1902. The first and most violent was the so-called "Ikhwan revolt" of the late 1920s. The Ikhwan were bedouin from major Najdi tribes such as 'Utayba and Mutayr who had been religiously indoctrinated and trained as a military force for use in the territorial expansion of the nascent Saudi state. When the expansion reached the border of territories controlled by the British colonial power, King 'Abd al-'Aziz called for an end to further military campaigns. The Ikhwan, who had already grown critical of 'Abd al-'Aziz because of his use of modern technology and his interaction with Westerners, were outraged by the abandonment of jihad for reasons of realpolitik. Some of the Ikhwan leaders also had personal political ambitions that were thwarted by Ibn Sa'ud.¹¹ They refused to lay down their weapons and instead rebelled against their king. After a series of clashes, the bedouin fighting force, led by Sultan b. Bijad and Faysal Al Dawish, shaykhs of the 'Utayba and Mutayr tribes, was crushed at the battle of Sbila in 1929. Ikhwan members who had remained loyal were later absorbed into the national guard.

The 1950s and 1960s witnessed a few episodes of leftist and communist unrest in the kingdom, which reinforced the regime's conviction that a reliance on religious forces was the best means of social control. The accession to the throne of the pan-Islamist King Faisal in 1964 and the dynamics of the Arab

Cold War further increased the budgets and the influence of the religious establishment and Islamic organizations in Saudi Arabia. This created a context favorable to the development of local brands of Islamism, from which later movements of political–religious opposition would emerge.

At this time, two different types of Islamism developed in Saudi Arabia. One was pragmatic, political, and elitist and became known as the Islamic awakening (*al-sahwa al-Islamiyya*), or just the Sahwa. This represented the mainstream of the Saudi Islamist movement. On its margins emerged an isolationist, pietistic, and lower-class Islamist phenomenon, which can be termed "rejectionist" or "neo-Salafi." From the 1960s to the 1990s the two strains coexisted, representing relatively distinct ideological approaches and sociological phenomena, although the former remained politically and numerically more significant. The Sahwa developed primarily on university campuses after the arrival, from the late 1950s onward, of large numbers of members of the Muslim Brotherhood fleeing persecution in countries such as Egypt and Syria. These individuals—many of whom were academics or well-trained professionals—rapidly became the backbone of the newly established Saudi education and media sectors. It was partly through their impulse that the Sahwa gained momentum in Saudi universities in the 1970s and 1980s, before spearheading the reformist Islamist opposition of the early 1990s. Ideologically, the Sahwa represented a blend of the traditional Wahhabi outlook (mainly on social issues) and the more contemporary Muslim Brotherhood approach (especially on political issues). Politically, representatives of the Sahwa have sought to reform the state's policies without ever straightforwardly questioning the state's legitimacy.[12]

However, it is from the other Islamist strain—the rejectionist one—that Juhayman's movement emerged in the 1970s. In 1961, the Islamic University of Medina was set up under the leadership of Grand Mufti Muhammad b. Ibrahim Al al-Shaykh and the later well-known 'Abd al-'Aziz b. Baz.[13] Both were eager to inspire a broader Wahhabi movement in the Hijaz, which for decades had enjoyed relative cultural and religious autonomy. They therefore encouraged their students to engage in proselytizing (da'wa) and enforcement of religious laws (hisba).

These developments coincided with the arrival of new ideological influences on the Medinan religious scene, in particular that of Muhammad Nasir al-Din al-Albani (1914–99). Al-Albani was a Syria-based scholar of Albanian origin who had been invited by 'Abd al-'Aziz b. Baz, then vice-president of the Islamic University of Medina, to teach there in 1961. Al-Albani had become famous in Syria for identifying himself with the medieval school of thought known as the ahl al-hadith (i.e., "the people of hadith"), which he claimed to revive. The ahl al-hadith had become known in the eighth century for opposing the use of reason in religious rulings, insisting that only the Sunna was to provide answers for matters not explicitly treated in the Qur'an. Their scholars, therefore, developed a particular interest in the collection and the study of hadith. Of the four canonical law schools that were to emerge a century later, only the Hanbali school followed a strict ahl al-hadith line. The late Hanbalis, however, increasingly tended to imitate (taqlid) former rulings by members of their school, instead of practicing their own interpretation (ijtihad) based on the Qur'an and the Sunna. This was one of al-Albani's main reproaches of the Wahhabis, who claimed ijtihad but tended to act as Hanbalis, and, therefore, as madhhabis (i.e., those who follow a particular school of jurisprudence). Al-Albani rejected all the schools of jurisprudence, calling for direct and exclusive reliance on the Qur'an and the Sunna. He also reproached the Wahhabis for not caring enough about hadith. He held his own views on the authenticity and readings of certain hadith, and, therefore, his rulings sometimes ran counter to well-established—and especially Wahhabi—beliefs, notably on ritual issues. In his well-known book *Sifat salat al-Nabi* [Characteristics of the Prophet's prayer], al-Albani presented several peculiar views on Islamic rituals that proved to be controversial among other Saudi scholars. Some say these controversies led to his expulsion from Medina in 1963, although the exact circumstances of his departure are unclear. Al-Albani nevertheless maintained a close relationship with the Saudi *'ulama* throughout his life, particularly with Ibn Baz. The teachings of the charismatic al-Albani had a strong impact on the Saudi religious scene, not least because they formed the ideological basis for the pietistic organization from which Juhayman's rebels emerged, namely, al-Jama'a al-Salafiyya al-Muhtasiba.

Al-Jama'a al-Salafiyya al-Muhtasiba

The group known as al-Jama'a al-Salafiyya al-Muhtasiba (JSM) took shape in Medina in the mid-1960s. It was formed by a small group of religious students who for some time had been proselytizing in the city's poorer neighborhoods.[14] Having been influenced by al-Albani, they were driven by a general conviction that mainstream schools and tendencies in the Muslim world at the time—including the official Wahhabism of the Saudi religious establishment—needed to be purified of innovations and misperceptions. They also acted to counter the growing influence of other groups on the religious scene in early 1970s Medina, particularly Jama'at al-Tabligh, but also the Muslim Brotherhood.[15] Both of these aims—promoting a purified Wahhabism and providing an alternative to existing forms of Islamic activism—were shared by some of the most prominent religious scholars in Medina at the time, such as 'Abd al-'Aziz b. Baz and Abu Bakr al-Jaza'iri.[16] The founding members of the JSM developed personal contacts with these scholars and considered Ibn Baz their shaykh.

The formation of the JSM was prompted by an episode known among the members as "the breaking of the pictures" (*taksir al-suwar*), which occurred in approximately 1965. The proselytizers had gradually come to see it as their duty to enforce religious obligations and regulations in certain parts of Medina. This included destroying pictures and photographs in public spaces. In the early 1960s, there was friction and were even minor clashes in Medina between these zealous conservatives and local residents.[17] This vigilantism went unnoticed or ignored until a group of young activists were caught smashing a large number of display windows showing female mannequins in the center of Medina. Having inflicted serious damage on commercial property, the perpetrators were arrested and imprisoned for approximately a week.[18] This confrontation with the police inspired the main activists to intensify and coordinate their efforts. Not long after this incident, they decided to set up an organization under the name al-Jama'a al Salafiyya (the Salafi group). They approached Ibn Baz to ask for his approval. He greeted the initiative and suggested that they add the qualification *al-muhtasiba* ("which practices *hisba*") to the name of their group.[19] Ibn Baz thus became the official spiritual guide (*murshid*) of al-Jama'a al-Salafiyya al-Muhtasiba and appointed Abu Bakr al-Jaza'iri as his deputy.[20] The JSM had no official executive leader but was governed by a consultative council (*majlis al-shura*) of five or six members, including four of the founding members and al-Jaza'iri.

The group gradually stepped up its activities and attracted an increasingly large number of followers in Medina. In the early 1970s, they set themselves up in a purpose-built two-story building known as Bayt al-Ikhwan (House of the

Brotherhood) located in the poor neighborhood of al-Hara al-Sharqiyya in Medina, an area known for the strict conservatism of its residents. Bayt al-Ikhwan became the natural assembly point and administrative center for the JSM, as well as a forum for daily classes and weekly conferences. It was administered by Ahmad Hasan al-Muʿallim, a close friend of Juhayman and a former Yemeni student at the Islamic university.

Over time, the JSM's organizational structure became increasingly large and complex. Special administrative groups were set up to coordinate practical matters. One group (initially headed by Juhayman) specialized in organizing members' travels, another in the reception of guests, and a third in organizing trips to the villages for "wandering travelers" (al-musafirun al-jawwalun) to preach and recruit new members.[21] The JSM encouraged its adherents to set up similar communities in other cities around the kingdom. By 1976, the JSM had followers based in practically all major Saudi cities, including Mecca, Riyadh, Jedda, Taif, Ha'il, Abha, Dammam, and Burayda. All branches had a local leader or contact person. Some branches, like the one in Mecca, were also based in purpose-built houses.[22]

To determine the socioeconomic profiles of JSM members, we asked al-Huzaymi to provide us with as much information as he remembered on members of the group. This, combined with other sources, allowed us to gather basic demographic data on thirty-five individuals, and enabled us to make a few important overall observations.[23] First, it seems that most members were young, unmarried men. Some members did have families, but no women played any direct role in the organization. Adherents covered a relatively wide age span—from late teens to late forties—but the majority seem to have been in their mid-twenties. Second, most JSM members came from those who had been marginalized or discriminated against. Many were recently urbanized young men with a *badawi* (translated as bedouin)[24] background.[25] Historically, tribes have largely been considered the losers of the Saudi modernization process, both in political terms (at the collective level) and in economic terms (at the individual level).[26] Other JSM members were residents of foreign origin (with and without Saudi citizenship), mostly from Yemen.[27] It is no secret that foreigners have long suffered a degree of social and political, if not necessarily economic, discrimination in Saudi society.[28] The refusal of JSM members, for ideological reasons, to take government positions often contributed to their marginalization. They were, therefore, often described by outside observers at the time as "unemployed," "shop assistants," or "students."[29]

Ideologically, the JSM initially focused on moral and religious reform, not on politics. In its view, Islam had been corrupted by the introduction of reprehensible innovations (*bid'a*) in religious practice and by society's deviation from religious principles. They advocated a return to a strict and literal reading of the Qur'an and hadith as the sole source of religious truth, and they rejected imitation (*taqlid*) of all subsequent scholars, including scholars that are revered in the Wahhabi tradition, such as Ibn Hanbal, Ibn Taymiyya, and Ibn 'Abd al-Wahhab. The JSM nevertheless held al-Albani in very high esteem and organized teaching or lecture sessions with him whenever he came from Jordan to Mecca on pilgrimage.[30] They also had links to the Pakistani Ahl-e Hadith through Shaykh Badi' al-Din al-Sindi, a Pakistani scholar based in Mecca who was one of the JSM's main religious references. There were also contacts between the JSM and the Egyptian Salafi group Ansar al-Sunna al-Muhammadiyya (Supporters of Muhammad's Tradition), whose monthly magazine, *al-Tawhid*, was widely read among JSM members and whose shaykhs would lecture at Bayt al-Ikhwan during their trips to Medina.[31]

The JSM's literal reading of religious texts led to an extreme social conservatism and to a rejectionist attitude toward many aspects of modernity. For example, they opposed the use of identity cards and passports because these denoted loyalty to an entity other than God. They were against images of living beings, not only on television and in photography but also on currency. More significantly, the JSM had peculiar views on ritual and prayer, which set the group apart from other religious communities at the time. They shared many of the interpretations presented by al-Albani in his book, *Sifat salat al-Nabi* [Characteristics of the Prophet's prayer].[32] For example, they argued that the condition for breaking the fast during Ramadan was not the setting of the sun but the disappearance of sunlight, hence fast could be broken during Ramadan in a room with closed windows. They considered it permissible to pray while wearing sandals, and caused a certain amount of friction with fellow worshippers in the Prophet's Mosque in Medina. Bayt al-Ikhwan, therefore, contained a mosque where the group's adherents could worship according to their own peculiar practices. Unlike other mosques, it contained no niche (*mihrab*), because the JSM considered this an innovation (*bid'a*).

The unorthodox practices of the JSM worried Medinan scholars who had initially been sympathetic to the group. Muqbil al-Wadi'i, one of the JSM shaykhs, recalls being summoned by two senior Medina-based scholars, 'Atiyya Salim and 'Umar Falata, who questioned him on "twelve issues" which they deemed problematic.[33] The relations reached a breaking point in the late summer of 1977, when a group of senior *'ulama* led by Abu Bakr al-Jaza'iri—Ibn Baz had already left Medina at this point—visited Bayt al-Ikhwan in the hope of convincing the members to relinquish their practices. They held a meeting on the roof, during which Shaykh al-Jaza'iri clashed with the hard-line Juhayman al-'Utaybi.[34] The meeting ended with a split in the JSM: a minority—

including most of the historical leaders of the group—declared their loyalty to al-Jaza'iri and left Bayt al-Ikhwan, whereas a majority—comprising the youngest and most hotheaded members—rallied around Juhayman and insisted on continuing their work. Muqbil al-Wadi'i recounts how he tried to mediate, unsuccessfully, between the two factions. Al-Wadi'i writes that Juhayman was extremely distrustful and openly accused fellow JSM members—including founding members of the group, such as Sulayman al-Shtawi—of being police informers.[35] After the rooftop episode, Juhayman was left as the only senior person and the natural leader of the smaller and radicalized JSM. From then on, Juhayman's name became synonymous with the organization, and he and his followers simply referred to themselves as *Ikhwan* (brothers).

Juhayman's Ikhwan

When Juhayman b. Muhammad b. Sayf al-'Utaybi rose to the fore as an Islamist leader in the mid-1970s, he was already in his forties. Many questions remain about his early life. We do know that he was born in the early- or mid-1930s to a bedouin family in the Ikhwan settlement (*hijra*) of Sajir in the western part of the Najd region. Juhayman's family belonged to the Suqur branch of the large 'Utayba tribe. The young Juhayman was raised in a traditional bedouin environment. His grandfather, Sayf al-Dhan, was a horseman who participated widely in bedouin raids before the emergence of the Saudi state under King 'Abd al-'Aziz.[36] Contrary to claims by some historians, Juhayman's grandfather was not involved in the Ikhwan revolts. According to al-Huzaymi, it was Juhayman's father, Muhammad b. Sayf, who fought beside the rebel leader Sultan b. Bijad. Muhammad survived the battle of Sbila in 1929 and lived until 1972. Juhayman was proud of his father's exploits and was keen to evoke the memory of the old Ikhwan to his comrades in the JSM.[37] Juhayman left school very early. Al-Huzaymi says Juhayman himself admitted having completed only the fourth year of primary school. The widespread rumors of his illiteracy seem to be at least partially true. Al-Huzaymi says he never saw Juhayman write—and that the latter's spoken classical Arabic was poor and colored by bedouin dialect. The so-called "letters of Juhayman" were dictated to a friend acting as a scribe, al-Huzaymi says. However, as Joseph Kechichian has rightly pointed out, Juhayman was clearly not illiterate, given his command of religious literature and his authorship of several works in classical Arabic.[38] Therefore, a likely explanation is that Juhayman was dyslexic, in other words, academically and linguistically able, but uncomfortable with writing.

Juhayman spent the bulk of his working life in the national guard. By most accounts, he joined in 1955 and left in late 1973, although he may have left earlier.[39] His reasons for leaving the guard are unclear; some sources say he left voluntarily, whereas others suggest that he was dismissed in humiliating circumstances. After leaving, he moved to Medina, yet again for unknown reasons. Lacking formal school qualifications, Juhayman never enrolled in the Islamic University of Medina, as many historians have suggested. However, he did attend classes for a period at Dar al-Hadith, an old institution specializing in the teaching of hadith, and affiliated with the University of Medina. It was during that time that he joined the JSM. Juhayman rose to prominence in the JSM primarily because of his charisma, age, and tribal pedigree. It was particularly his readiness to openly criticize the 'ulama that drew the admiration of younger members of the organization.[40] After the rooftop episode and the split in the JSM, Juhayman came to dominate the group to the extent that, according to al-Huzaymi, Juhayman's Ikhwan had many of the traits of a personality cult. The young members competed for Juhayman's favor and were socially ranked according to their relationship with and proximity to the leader. Juhayman, in return, punished those who dared to argue with him by ignoring them, leaving them socially excluded from the group.[41]

In December 1977, shortly after the rooftop episode, the authorities, who had received reports of the group's radicalization through former members, decided to take action.[42] Police planned to raid Bayt al-Ikhwan and arrest Juhayman along with his associates. Juhayman, however, received a tip-off about the coming raid some hours in advance by a police insider from the 'Utayba tribe.[43] Juhayman left Bayt al-Ikhwan immediately with two aides, one of whom was Nasir al-Huzaymi. He sought refuge in the desert, where police jurisdiction was weaker and his bedouin allies more numerous than in the cities. Juhayman stayed in the desert for almost two years, and was not seen in public again until the seizure of the Grand Mosque in Mecca. Meanwhile, around thirty people in Medina were arrested and imprisoned for six weeks under accusation of weapons possession. In the days that followed, leading Juhayman associates in other cities were also detained, although in smaller numbers.[44]

During these two years, Juhayman led a peripatetic life in the northern desert regions, in a triangle-shaped area between Ha'il, Burayda, and Hafr al-Batin. He was accompanied at any given time by a small entourage of three to five people, but he maintained contact with the rest of his followers. The police were continuously on his trail, and there are many anecdotes about Juhayman's secret ventures into inhabited areas. Shortly after his escape into the desert, Juhayman wanted to visit his mother in his hometown of Sajir but was prevented from doing so at the last minute when he received a tip-off that the police were keeping her under surveillance. At one stage, Juhayman suffered from a toothache, and after a long and painful wait, his aides managed to find a dentist who would not inform the authorities. Meanwhile, secret meetings for his followers were held in remote locations on a regular basis, although usually without Juhayman being present.[45]

After the police crackdown on Bayt al-Ikhwan, Juhayman no longer had a forum in which to gather followers and communicate his ideas. Juhayman's desert existence, therefore, marked the starting point of his ideological production. He started recording his ideas on cassette tapes and in pamphlets. None of the tape recordings is available today, but his pamphlets have survived.[46] They offer important insights into his thinking. However, there has been much confusion about the total number, exact titles, and real authorship.[47] Although these pamphlets are commonly referred to as the "letters of Juhayman," only eight of them were actually signed by him, and, as he was uncomfortable with writing, these were dictated to his associates Muhammad al-Qahtani (the future Mahdi)[48] and Ahmad al-Mu'allim, who transcribed them. It now seems clear that there are twelve letters in total and that they were published in batches of one, seven, and four. One is signed by al-Qahtani, one by a certain Yemeni named Hasan b. Muhsin al-Wahidi and two by *ahad talabat al-'ilm* (one of the seekers of knowledge), a pseudonym used by another Yemeni called Muhammad al-Saghir.[49]

Of interest, the letters were printed in Kuwait by the leftist newspaper *al-Tali'a* (the Vanguard), whose owners were sympathetic to what they interpreted as a potential working-class uprising in the Hijaz. A Kuwaiti JSM member named 'Abd al-Latif al-Dirbas used his family connections to negotiate a deal with the leftist publisher, then coordinated the transport and distribution of several thousand copies of Juhayman's pamphlets across Saudi Arabia. Nasir al-Huzaymi, who participated in the distribution of the first letter in Mecca, recalls several anecdotes regarding the publishing process. For example, the name of *al-Tali'a* press had accidentally been printed on the front page of each copy and had to be removed with scissors. Another problem emerged when the remarks from Shaykh Ibn Baz—to whom Juhayman had secretly presented the text for approval—arrived only after the text had been printed. Hence, Ibn Baz's remarks had to be manually rubber-stamped onto each and every copy.[50]

The first letter was distributed in several cities simultaneously on 31 August 1978.[51] The group of texts known as "the seven letters" was printed shortly afterward and distributed during the hajj in November 1978. A few months later came another group of four letters.[52] The "seven" and the "four" letters were also presented to Ibn Baz, who allegedly agreed with their content, except for the fact that they specifically targeted Saudi Arabia.[53] Their distribution angered the regime, which ordered new arrests within the JSM. Among the individuals targeted was Muqbil al-Wadi'i, who was accused of being their author. He was released after three months and expelled to Yemen.[54]

The letters were not only circulated across Saudi Arabia, but also in Kuwait, where the JSM gathered a relatively large following. A good indication of its growing presence in Kuwait is the fact that 'Abd al-Rahman 'Abd al-Khaliq, the leading figure of the mainstream Salafi movement in the Emirate, wrote a series of articles in the Kuwaiti newspaper al-Watan in late 1978 refuting Juhayman's ideas.[55] It is also worth noting that, on the day of the storming of the Grand Mosque, some of Juhayman's letters were distributed in Kuwaiti mosques.[56]

Juhayman's letters are written in a relatively monotonous religious language and do not reveal a particularly clear political doctrine. In the most political of his letters, "al-Imara wa-l-bay'a wa-l-ta'a," [The state, allegiance and obedience], Juhayman accuses the Saudi regime of "making religion a means to guarantee their worldly interests, putting an end to jihad, paying allegiance to the Christians [America] and bringing over Muslims evil and corruption." He added that in any case, the Al Sa'ud's non-Qurayshi origin (i.e., not descendants from the Prophet Muhammad's tribe) excluded them from the right to Islamic leadership. This led him to the conclusion that the *bay'a* (oath of allegiance) that unites Saudis to their rulers is invalid (*batila*) and that obeying them is no longer compulsory, especially on those very issues where their behavior and orders contradict God's word. Therefore, he called for his followers to keep away from state institutions by resigning if they were civil servants or by leaving school or university if they were still students.

He warned, however, that pronouncing *takfir* (excommunication) upon rulers is prohibited as long as they call themselves Muslims. He thus differentiated between the state as an institution, which he deemed illegitimate and un-Islamic, and individual members of the government—whom he refused to excommunicate. Likewise, Juhayman was extremely critical of the official religious establishment as an institution, but he was more careful in expressing opinions about specific scholars such as Ibn Baz.

On a more doctrinal level, Juhayman revived several important concepts from the writings of hardline Wahhabi scholars from the nineteenth century such as Sulayman b. 'Abdallah al-Shaykh and Hamad b. 'Atiq.[57] The first concept was that of *millat Ibrahım* (the community of Abraham), which is an allegory for the true Islamic community that has disassociated from all forms of impiety. The second was *awthaq 'ura al-iman* (the strongest bonds of faith), meaning the links that unite Muslims with each other and impose on them mutual solidarity. Both concepts converged in the principle of *al-wala' wa-l-bara'* (allegiance [to fellow Muslims] and dissociation [from infidels]), which Juhayman made the defining principle for correct Islamic behavior. Another important element in Juhayman's ideology is that of the coming of the Mahdi. The first of his "seven letters" is devoted entirely to this theme.[58] This text presents all the authentic hadiths about the Mahdi, correlating them with recent events in the modern history of the Arabian Peninsula to demonstrate the imminence of the Mahdi's coming. In the same pamphlet, he wrote that "we have dedicated all our efforts to this issue for the past eight years."[59] According to al-Huzaymi, the issue of the Mahdi had indeed been talked about in the JSM all along, but it only became a central part of Juhayman's discourse in mid 1978, after his escape into the desert. In late 1978, Juhayman declared that it had been confirmed to him in a dream that his companion Muhammad al-Qahtani was the Mahdi.[60] One of the reasons why al-Qahtani was identified as such was that he possessed several of the Mahdi's attributes as described in the corresponding hadiths. First, he was called Muhammad b. 'Abdallah, as was the Prophet. Second, he claimed to belong to the *ashraf*, the Prophet's lineage.[61] Third, his physical appearance was allegedly in conformity with the descriptions of the Mahdi in religious tradition.[62] The designation of al-Qahtani created a second major split in the organization. Many members, including Nasir al-Huzaymi, were unconvinced by the messianic talk and left the movement for good. It was this remaining core of Juhayman's followers who carried out one of the most spectacular operations in the history of militant Islamism, the seizure of the Grand Mosque in Mecca.

On 20 November 1979, the first day of the fifteenth century of the Islamic calendar, a group of approximately 300 rebels led by Juhayman al-'Utaybi stormed and seized control of the Grand Mosque in Mecca, the holiest place in Islam. Their aim was to have al-Qahtani consecrated as the Mahdi between the black stone corner of the Ka'ba (*al-rukn al-aswad*) and Ibrahim's station of prayer (*al-maqam*), as tradition requires.

The militants barricaded themselves in the compound, taking thousands of worshippers hostage and awaiting the approach of a hostile army from the north, as promised by the eschatological tradition.[63] The situation developed into a two-week siege that left a hitherto unknown number of people dead and exposed serious gaps in the Saudi crisis-response capability. The timing of the attack was most likely determined by Juhayman's belief in the Sunni tradition of the "renewer of the century" (*mujaddid al-qarn*), according to which a great scholar will appear at the beginning of each *hijri* century.[64] Juhayman may have attempted to blend the renewer tradition with the Sunni mahdist tradition and thus concluded that the dawn of the new century was a propitious moment to consecrate al-Qahtani as the Mahdi.[65] The Mecca rebellion was thus entirely unrelated to the Shi'i uprising, which occurred almost simultaneously in the Eastern Province.[66] However, the occurrence of two internal uprisings in the space of a few months in 1979, as well as key international events such as the Iranian Revolution and the Soviet invasion of Afghanistan, certainly affected the outlook of the Saudi political leadership.

Nasir al-Huzaymi, who had extensive conversations in prison with surviving rebels, says that Juhayman's group had begun collecting weapons in late 1978, approximately a year before the attack. The main coordinator of weapons acquisition was Muhammad al-Qahtani's brother Sa'id. He bought arms from Yemeni smugglers with money raised by wealthier members of the group. In the months preceding the attack, they conducted weapons training on various locations in the countryside outside Mecca and Medina.[67] The rebels knew in advance that their operation might turn into a siege, and therefore they placed approximately a week's worth of food supplies (dried milk, dates, and bread) in the basement of the mosque complex shortly before the operation. Many also brought radios, expecting to hear news of the approach and subsequent engulfment of the hostile army from the north as promised by tradition. Al-Huzaymi's account also describes a rebel group perplexed by the death of Muhammad al-Qahtani on the third day of the siege. Some started having second thoughts, while others obeyed Juhayman's orders not to acknowledge al-Qahtani's death. Even years after the events, some JSM followers continued to believe that the Mahdi was still alive.[68]

On 4 December 1979, Saudi authorities regained control of the sanctuary with the assistance of three French special-forces officers led by Captain Paul Barril. The rebels were tried and sentenced with lightning speed. At dawn on 9 January 1980, sixty-three people were executed in eight different cities around the kingdom. The list of convicts, which had been published two days earlier in the Saudi press, included forty-one Saudis, ten Egyptians, six South Yemenis, three Kuwaitis, a North Yemeni, an Iraqi, and a Sudanese.[69] However, the people executed do not necessarily represent the most prominent members in Juhayman's organization, but rather the individuals who fought most fiercely in the final stages of the siege and survived. Al-Huzaymi explains that prisoners underwent a quick medical examination to determine who would be executed. Those with bruises or pains in their shoulders were assumed to have fired upon the security forces and were punished by death. Those not executed received long prison sentences. Saudi police also arrested a large number of people across the kingdom who had been involved with the JSM or Juhayman's Ikhwan at some stage. Those who escaped arrest (or were released early) sought refuge in a variety of locations. Many went abroad, particularly to Kuwait, but also to Yemen. Others sought a quiet existence in Riyadh or in conservative cities in the Najd, such as al-Zulfi and al-Rass.[70] The bedouins who had helped Juhayman were largely unaffected by the crackdown, and many of them are still present in the northern desert regions. Within a few months of the Mecca event, Juhayman's organization was almost completely dismantled, at least in Saudi Arabia. The Kuwaiti branch of the movement survived and remained active until the end of the 1980s, albeit in a form closer to the original JSM than to Juhayman's Ikhwan.[71]

The Mecca event shook the regime, which was concentrating its political control on leftist groups and had not expected its foes to come from religious circles. It decided, however, that only a reinforcement of the powers of the religious establishment and its control on Saudi society would prevent such unrest from happening again. Ironically, it was the other main Islamist current, the more institutionally integrated Sahwa, which benefited from these new policies and grew stronger throughout the 1980s, until it openly confronted the regime in the early 1990s.

Interpreting Juhayman's Movement

Juhayman's movement has been the subject of a significant number of analyses, some of them outwardly political, others overly simplistic. One explanation, heard particularly—but not only—from Saudi officials at the time, is that Juhayman's movement was the product of foreign ideological influences, mainly from Egyptian groups such as Shukri Mustafa's Jama'at al-Muslimin (Society of Muslims), commonly known as al-Takfir wa-l-Hijra (Excommunication and Emigration). These claims relied in part on the fact that many of the people arrested after the event were Egyptian citizens, as were ten of the sixty-three executed rebels. It is indeed beyond doubt that there were Egyptian al-Takfir wa-l-Hijra members in Saudi Arabia in the mid-1970s.[72] However, al-Huzaymi insists that the Egyptian element in the JSM was negligible and that most of the arrested Egyptians had joined the rebellion immediately before the seizure of the mosque. He admits that in 1976–77 there were a handful of individuals in the JSM who held *takfiri* positions, but they changed their minds after Shaykh al-Albani sat down with them during one of his visits to Medina and convinced them otherwise.[73] The most important foreign ideological influence on the JSM came not from Egyptian extremist groups but from al-Albani's *ahl al-hadith* school of thought. If the JSM had contact with foreign organizations, it was primarily the Pakistani Ahl-e Hadith and the Egyptian Ansar al-Sunna al-Muhammadiyya, both of which are apolitical, nonviolent movements. Hence these foreign contacts do not in any way explain the political radicalization and activism of Juhayman, whose movement must be understood primarily as a domestic Saudi phenomenon.

Among the interpretations of the Mecca episode found most often in academic literature is the view that Juhayman's rebellion was essentially a modern replay of the 1920s Ikhwan revolt.[74] The memory of the original Ikhwan certainly had an influence on Juhayman, who liked to tell his father's stories at JSM gatherings. There are also a few references to the early Ikhwan in Juhayman's letters, for example, he writes,

> We wish to clear of all suspicions our "Ikhwan" brothers who conducted jihad in the name of God and were faithful to it, while this state and its evil scholars presented them as Kharijites, to the extent that one can now find people to whom the issue is so unclear that they don't even ask God to grant them His mercy.[75]

However, many of the JSM's members were not bedouin, and many among the bedouin in the JSM did not come from tribes that were prominent in the first Ikhwan revolt. It would, therefore, be far too simplistic to explain Juhayman's rebellion as a resurgence of old tribal grievances against the Al Sa'ud. Restoring the honor of the first Ikhwan was only one minor aspect of the group's message. Despite their reactionary positions, the JSM and Juhayman's Ikhwan were essentially a modern phenomenon to be understood within the context of 1970s Saudi Arabia, a society undergoing rapid socioeconomic change and a steady process of politicization.

Another frequently heard explanation is that Juhayman and his followers were apocalyptics who had drifted so far in their belief in the Mahdi that they had lost their sense of political rationality. It seems relatively clear now that Juhayman's personal belief in the Mahdi was genuine and that this was indeed a major factor behind the takeover of the Grand Mosque. At the same time, Nasir al-Huzaymi insists that some of Juhayman's companions did not believe in the messianic dimension of his ideology. These individuals chose to stay because they felt a strong sense of loyalty to the charismatic Juhayman and to the group or because they were convinced of other aspects of the ideology, such as the need for a religious and moral purification of society.[76] Moreover, reducing Juhayman's Ikhwan to a messianic sect would ignore the political dimension of Juhayman's discourse as well as the question of why this movement gathered such strength at this particular point in time. It seems, then, that we need to understand Juhayman's group as being simultaneously messianic and political.

A last interpretation, favored by the Arab left at the time of the attack, is that the Mecca event represented a "people's rebellion," in which the disenfranchised Saudi working class rose up against the rich Saudi elite. Days after the event, the Arab Socialist Labour Party in the Arabian Peninsula expressed its support for the rebels. Shortly afterward, Nasir al-Sa'id, the historic leader of the Arabian Peninsula People's Union, described the attack as part of a "people's revolution" aimed at establishing a republic and adopting democratic freedoms.[77] He claimed that fighting had been going on in other places, such as Tabuk, Medina, Najran, and parts of Najd—a version of the events adopted by Alexei Vassiliev, among others.[78] Al-Sa'id's allegation seemed so well informed that it caught the attention of Saudi authorities, and on 17 December 1979 he mysteriously disappeared in Beirut, never to reappear. Today, it is clear that his claims were not true.[79] However, the leftists were, to some extent, right in pointing out that the rebels were for the most part poor and disenfranchised. As noted earlier, Juhayman's Brotherhood, as the JSM before it, drew most of its members from the politically, economically, and socially marginalized sections of Saudi society, particularly recently sedentary nomadic tribes and residents of foreign origin.

As we have seen from this discussion, there is no simple explanation for the emergence of Juhayman's movement. A first and important step in the analysis is to distinguish between the JSM on the one hand and Juhayman's Brotherhood on the other. The emergence of the JSM seems to be linked to three important societal changes in Saudi Arabia in the 1960s and 1970s. The first was the slow but steady push toward increased social conservatism from a religious establishment that sensed that it was losing its grip on an increasingly liberal society. The second was the arrival of new ideological currents that provided alternatives to the established political and religious order. The third was the socioeconomic tensions resulting from Saudi Arabia's rapid modernization process. As for the emergence of Juhayman's Brotherhood, it seems to have followed a classic pattern of group radicalization, whereby a small faction breaks out of a larger and more moderate organization after a process of politicization and internal debate. After the break, the behavior of the radicalized faction is more determined by ideology and charismatic leadership than by structural socioeconomic and political factors.

Juhayman's Legacy

It has long been assumed that Juhayman al-'Utaybi and his movement represent an exceptional and rather short-lived phenomenon whose influence on the subsequent history of Saudi Islamism has been rather limited. However, as we shall see, there are many indications that the memory of Juhayman has been kept alive in certain Islamist circles until today and that his ideology has inspired periodic attempts at reviving his movement.

Most prominent among Juhayman's intellectual heirs is Abu Muhammad al-Maqdisi (aka 'Isam Barqawi, b. 1959), a radical Islamist ideologue of Palestinian origin who grew up in Kuwait. In the early 1980s, he started frequenting Islamist circles in Kuwait, where he came in contact with the local JSM branch, whose ranks had swelled with the arrival of remnants of the Saudi JSM in 1980.[80] He became friends with Juhayman's former associate 'Abd al-Latif al-Dirbas, who returned from Saudi Arabia after being released from prison.[81] In 1981 or 1982, al-Maqdisi went to Medina to study religion, during which time he made many contacts with former Juhayman sympathizers across the kingdom.

Al-Maqdisi's writings were heavily influenced by Juhayman's ideology and contained numerous references to Juhayman.[82] However, al-Maqdisi was more radical than Juhayman on several issues. Most notably, al-Maqdisi did not hesitate to pronounce *takfir* upon Muslim rulers. In 1989, he wrote a book, *al-Kawashif al-jaliyya fi kufr al-dawla al-Sa'udiyya* [The obvious proofs of the Saudi state's impiety], in which he praised Juhayman, while adding that "unfortunately, he [Juhayman] considered that rebelling against these rulers, whatever they may do, ... is contrary to the Sunna. ... Very unfortunately, he considered this government to be Muslim."[83]

Abu Muhammad al-Maqdisi did not remain with the JSM for long as he kept arguing with them over the issue of *takfir*.

Instead, he went to Peshawar in 1985 to join the Arab–Afghan community, and he subsequently became one of the leading ideologues of the so-called Salafi–Jihadi movement. However, he preserved his admiration for Juhayman, and in the late 1980s he traveled regularly to Saudi Arabia, where he paid visits to former friends of Juhayman in the Saudi desert.[84] In the early 1990s, al-Maqdisi left Peshawar and settled in Jordan, where he became the spiritual leader of a Jordanian militant community. He was imprisoned in 1995 but has continued to write from his cell. Recently, al-Maqdisi has attracted much attention for his open criticism of the activities in Iraq of his former pupil, Abu Mus'ab al-Zarqawi.

The early 1990s witnessed a revival of Juhayman's ideas in certain Islamist circles in Saudi Arabia. The authors of the current book learned of the existence of a small community of young Saudi Islamists in Riyadh in the early 1990s who saw themselves as the continuation of Juhayman's movement.[85] The community had taken shape around a core of three or four individuals in their early twenties who considered society in general, and state education in particular, corrupt.[86] They broke with their families and set themselves up in an apartment in the Shubra area of al-Suwaydi district in Riyadh where they could study religion on their own. Their apartment, which aimed at recreating Juhayman's Bayt al-Ikhwan, was known as Bayt Shubra, and it soon became a meeting place for like-minded youth. Although only five to ten people lived there at any one time, many more attended informal lessons or dropped by for discussion and socializing.

The residents of Bayt Shubra did not consider themselves part of an organization, but rather "seekers of religious knowledge" (talabat 'ilm). In their view, this knowledge could not be found among the shaykhs of the religious establishment, whom they considered corrupt, nor among the leaders of the Sahwa, whom they saw as too political. Instead they looked to the writings of Juhayman, al-Maqdisi, and nineteenth-century Wahhabi theologians such as Sulayman b. 'Abdallah Al al-Shaykh. The residents of Bayt Shubra greatly admired Juhayman and saw themselves as his ideological successors. Because none of them was old enough to have known Juhayman personally, they sought out former members of the JSM in various parts of the country, particularly among the bedouin in the desert.[87] They also invited former JSM members in Riyadh to lecture in Bayt Shubra. Abu Muhammad al-Maqdisi himself visited the apartment during one of his visits to Saudi Arabia.[88] The Bayt Shubra residents adopted the JSM's extreme social conservatism, strong emphasis on ritual matters, as well as its skepticism toward the state and its institutions. Juhayman's mahdist ideas, however, do not seem to have been particularly important in Bayt Shubra, although some of its residents did accept those ideas and continued to believe that the Mahdi had not died in 1979.

Over time, however, the Bayt Shubra community grew more and more interested in politics, and its members eventually took more radical positions than Juhayman on several questions. Although the Bayt Shubra community was initially inward looking and apolitical, it was unable to avoid the political–religious debates of early 1990s Saudi Arabia, a time when the confrontation between the state and the Sahwa was at its most intense. The process of politicization introduced several disagreements, first (in 1992) on the issue of takfir of the royal family and later (around 1994) regarding takfir of the religious establishment. Eventually, the Bayt Shubra network split into several factions, each of which went its own way. The involvement of some former Bayt Shubra members in the 1995 Riyadh bombings led police to try to arrest the entire network. A few members managed to escape and found shelter with the very bedouin they had earlier gotten to know through their fascination with Juhayman. The others were marked by prison experience in different ways: some became more radical (several of them subsequently went to Afghanistan) whereas others began a process of soul-searching and went on to become liberal intellectuals.

Bayt Shubra was just one of many similar study circles that emerged throughout the kingdom at the time. Although these groups remained relatively marginal compared with the Sahwa—which was at its climax at this point—their very existence provides two significant new insights about Islamism in Saudi Arabia in the early 1990s. First, the ideology and example of Juhayman still had a significant appeal among young Saudis ten years after the Mecca event, and second, the Sahwa did not have a monopoly on the Islamist field. The Bayt Shubra residents shunned the Sahwa leaders (whom they saw as too interested in politics) and sought knowledge and inspiration from a different intellectual tradition. Among these communities, Bayt Shubra is historically the most interesting because many of its residents later became well-known figures. Some became prominent liberal writers, such as Mishari al-Dhayidi and 'Abdallah al-'Utaybi, whereas others made names as militants. Bayt Shubra's alumni include three of the four people convicted for the November 1995 Riyadh bombing as well as some of the senior militants involved in the terrorist campaign launched in 2003.[89]

Conclusion: Juhayman al-'Utaybi and "Rejectionist Islamism" in Saudi Arabia

The study of Juhayman's legacy has shown that the influence of Juhayman on the development of Saudi Islamism is greater than generally assumed. Moreover, it has allowed us to trace the origins and the development of a particular intellectual tradition within Saudi Islamism; a tradition that categorically rejects the legitimacy of the state and its institutions and advocates withdrawal from the state's sphere. This intellectual tradition may be termed "rejectionist Islamism." Saudi rejectionist Islamism bears some similarity to other Islamist groups characterized by a withdrawal from society (such as Shukri Mustafa's Jama'at al-Muslimin in Egypt), but it is first and foremost a Saudi phenomenon to be understood within the dynamics of the Saudi political–religious landscape. Although the JSM and the Bayt Shubra network have no doubt been two of the most visible and politicized manifestations of this strain of Islamism, related communities have existed—and still exist—in Saudi Arabia.[90]

Identifying a rejectionist strain in Saudi Islamism also makes it easier to distinguish it from the better known phenomenon of "reformist Islamism," as exemplified by the Sahwa. The Sahwa consisted of prominent academics well integrated into the system, whereas the rejectionists attract the marginalized and avoid state education and employment altogether. They also clearly differ in their attitude toward the state: Sahwa Islamists such as Salman al-'Awda never openly question the state's legitimacy, they only criticize (although sometimes with virulence) its policies, which they strive to change through nonviolent, institutional means.

The 1980s witnessed the emergence of a third strain of Saudi Islamism: jihadism, which has its roots in the participation of thousands of Saudi youth in the Afghan jihad against the Soviet Union. The jihadists developed a highly militaristic culture that set them apart from other Islamist currents. They were also explicitly interested in politics, which rejectionists were not. However, Saudi jihadists were initially politicized and radicalized on issues of international politics, not on issues of domestic politics like their counterparts in other Arab countries. In 1990, Saudi jihadists were not openly critical of the Saudi state.

In the first half of the 1990s, jihadists and rejectionists started to mix, as was the case in the Bayt Shubra community.

Although they represented two different cultures—rejectionists being men of introspection and jihadists being men of action—their views converged on many important issues. Most importantly, they influenced each other, as many rejectionists became more interested in politics whereas the jihadists adopted the rejectionists' strong distaste for the Saudi state. By the late 1990s, many rejectionists had joined the jihadists and left for Afghanistan or elsewhere. By the early 2000s, the growing polarization of the Saudi Islamist field between reformists and jihadists left little room for the rejectionists. Juhayman's intellectual legacy had effectively been eclipsed—but the memory of his rebellion was more in vogue than ever.

CHAPTER 2

BETWEEN
REVOLUTION
AND APOLITICISM

*Nasir al-Din al-Albani
and his Impact on the Shaping of
Contemporary Salafism*

Stéphane Lacroix

WHEN, ON I OCTOBER 1999, Shaykh Muhammad Nasir al-Din al-Albani died at the venerable age of 85, virtually everyone in the world
of Salafi Islam was in mourning. In the eyes of many, he was
the third great contemporary figure of Salafism, after 'Abd al-
'Aziz b. Baz, the grand mufti of Saudi Arabia, deceased a few
months earlier, and his second-in-command within the Saudi
religious establishment, Muhammad b. 'Uthaymin. Salafi
newspapers, magazines, and websites celebrated the memory
of this son of an Albanian watchmaker who had become the
"traditionist[1] of the era" (*muhaddith al-'asr*),[2] recognized by all
as the greatest hadith scholar of his generation.

By confining al-Albani to the role of a brilliant technician of
hadith, the apparent consensus that took shape on this occasion
concealed the deeply multiform nature of a controversial

figure who, at least as much by the stands he took as through his religious expertise, contributed greatly to the structuring of Salafism since the 1960s. It is our intention here to restore the complexity of al-Albani's role by expounding on his career, his positions, and those of both his legitimate and illegitimate heirs.

Three Distinct Religious Traditions

In order to grasp the originality of al-Albani's thought, we first need to present the three religious traditions with which it is to various extents related, although in a complex and conflictual way.

Muslim Reformism

The first of these traditions is "Muslim Reformism." This term we shall take to mean the body of ideas developed from the end of the nineteenth century by a small number of Egyptian and Syrian intellectuals with a view to ending the decadence of the Muslim world through a renewal of Islam. Calling upon the Muslim world to throw off the fetters of servile imitation (*taqlid*) of precedent through a renewed interpretation (*ijtihad*), they were also distinguished by their defense of a certain Sunni orthodoxy following directly from the writings of the medieval jurist and theologian Taqi al-Din b. Taymiyya (1263–1328), characterized by a definite hostility to the practices of popular Islam and of Sufism. In this sense they shared certain ideas with the second religious tradition that here concerns us, i.e., Wahhabism, a doctrine of which, according to Henri Laoust, they professed a "watered-down"[3] version.

Wahhabism

The Wahhabi religious tradition derives from the intellectual heritage of the preacher Muhammad b. 'Abd al-Wahhab, who was himself a fervent reader of Ibn Taymiyya and, in 1744, "cofounder" with Muhammad b. Sa'ud of the first Saudi state. This tradition subsequently gave birth to the Saudi religious establishment, which considers itself its guardian.

The grand principles set forth by Ibn 'Abd al-Wahhab reflect his concern above all with theological questions and aim to purify the Islamic creed (*'aqida*), which he believed ought to be nothing but pure *tawhid* (divine oneness). He held that the faith of his contemporaries had so far deviated from the orthodoxy of their pious predecessors (*al-salaf al-salih*)[4] that the society in which he was living had fallen into a period of ignorance (*jahiliyya*) similar to the situation that prevailed before the advent of Islam. For it is not enough to proclaim *tawhid*, affirms Ibn 'Abd al-Wahhab, in order to be a true Muslim; one must also adhere to it in religious practice. Herein lies all of the differences that he established between, on the one hand, *tawhid al-rububiyya* (the affirmation that God is One) and *tawhid al-asma' wa-l-sifat* (the affirmation of the oneness of His names and His attributes) and, on the other hand, *tawhid al-uluhiyya* (the oneness of the object of worship).[5] The latter principle was at variance with different widespread religious practices in the Arabian peninsula of his time, such as the cult of saints (based on *tawassul*, or intercession) and Shi'ism, both of which Ibn 'Abd al-Wahhab denounced as forms of polytheist associationism (*shirk*).[6] It was essentially to counter these that Wahhabism was conceived.

However, while the theological positions of Ibn 'Abd al-Wahhab are clear, his legal positions (on *fiqh*, i.e., law)[7] are much less so, first and foremost because they are much less central to his doctrine.[8] His basic principle is that the only sources upon which a valid religious judgment can be based are the Qur'an, the Sunna[9] and the *ijma'* (consensus) of the pious predecessors. Theoretically, this comes down to a rejection of the *taqlid* (imitation) of the four canonical legal

schools, and to the establishment of *ijithad* (interpretation) as
the pillar of the law. In practice, nevertheless, Ibn ʿAbd al-
Wahhab continued to adhere to the Hanbali rules of exegesis,
which imply a very literal reading of the sacred texts. This is
what he emphasized in his letter to the *ʿulama* of Medina,[10] in
which, probably also seeking to prove thereby the orthodoxy
of his *daʿwa* (preaching), he went so far as to declare himself
a "non-innovating proponent" (*muttabiʿin ghayr mubtadiʿin*) of
the Hanbali school of law. In fact, it has been established that
Ibn ʿAbd al-Wahhab never delivered a novel legal opinion,
rather he restricted himself to a related *ijtihad* within the
compass of the Hanbali school. As is shown by Frank Vogel,[11]
this paradox between a declared *ijtihad* ideal and a legal practice
grounded largely in the Hanbali school has been a constant of
Wahhabism right up to our time. This paradox, as we shall
see, became one of the principal motors driving the conflict
between the Saudi religious establishment, guardian of the
Wahhabi tradition, and Muhammad Nasir al-Din al-Albani.

Ahl-e Hadith

The third religious tradition that concerns us here is that
of the Ahl-e Hadith ("the people of hadith") of the Indian
subcontinent. This movement took form in the 1860s around
two religious personalities, Nazir Husayn in Delhi, and
Siddiq Hasan Khan in Bhopal. The ideas of these two men
show strong similarities to the Wahhabi tradition. Like the
heirs of Ibn ʿAbd al-Wahhab, they were fiercely opposed
to Shiʿism and Sufism, which they considered dangerous
innovations. Also like them, they read the sacred texts very
literally, having recourse to *qiyas* (reasoning by analogy) only
in extremely limited circumstances. Finally, they were also
fervent readers of the work of Ibn Taymiyya.[12] The two
groups discovered how close their thinking was when their
paths crossed during the pilgrimage to Mecca. Subsequently,

some Wahhabi *'ulama* went to Bhopal and Delhi to study with their Indian colleagues.[13]

But while the tradition of the Ahl-e Hadith has certain important points in common with Wahhabism,[14] it differs radically in its methodology. Indeed, as opposed to the Wahhabis, the primary concern of the Ahl-e Hadith is with law (*fiqh*) rather than with creed (*'aqida*). Their intellectual starting point is a complete rejection of *taqlid* (imitation), particularly of the four canonical schools of jurisprudence, and a call to base all religious rulings exclusively on the Qur'an and the Sunna with no intermediary involved. This implies a special interest in hadith, which, alone, may provide answers to all legal questions for which the schools (especially the Shafi'i, the Maliki, and the Hanafi) relied on the *ra'y* (the opinion) of their founders and their disciples.[15] This had long been the position of the *ahl al-hadith* in the Middle Ages, during their disputes with the *ahl al-ra'y* (partisans of opinion), and the Indian movement sought to identify itself with them through their choice of name. One of the consequences of this alienation from the schools is a particular way of reading the sacred texts that entails a physical appearance and an outward way of praying that distinguishes the Ahl-e Hadith from other Muslims.

The earliest vector of the impact of the Ahl-e Hadith on the Saudi religious sphere was made up of those Wahhabi *'ulama* who, at the end of the nineteenth century, studied with the Indian shaykhs. The most emblematic of them is no doubt Sa'd b. 'Atiq (1850–1930), sent to India in 1881 by his father, the famous Wahhabi *'alim*, Hamad b. 'Atiq, who maintained a correspondence with Siddiq Hasan Khan. Sa'd, who spent nine years with the Ahl-e Hadith, later became a major religious figure of the third Saudi state, appointed by Ibn Sa'ud as a judge (*qadi*) in Riyadh and imam of the city's Grand Mosque,[16] an office that gave him great influence over the education of the young generation of Wahhabi *'ulama*. Among his students figured the young 'Abd al-'Aziz b. Baz, who was influenced early on by the teachings of the Ahl-e Hadith.

This Ahl-e Hadith influence, above all, highlighted the above-mentioned paradox in the Wahhabi attitude toward the legal schools. Intruding through the breach opened by the theoretical teaching of the rejection of *taqlid*, their doctrine led the Wahhabi *'ulama* to openly oppose Hanbali *fiqh*, among the scholars of whom Ibn Baz figured prominently. It was they who opened the way for Muhammad Nasir al-Din al-Albani, who became active in the kingdom from the 1960s on.

The Birth of Modern Salafism

"Salafism" has traditionally designated the practice of emulating the "pious predecessors" (*al-salaf al-salih*) by relying for religious rulings only on the Qur'an and the Sunna, as understood and interpreted by the first three generations of Muslims. In the modern Islamic debate, however, it is mainly used to denote Wahhabism itself as well as all the intellectual hybrids that sprouted from the Wahhabi substrate in Saudi Arabia throughout the twentieth century. In the climate of the policy of "Islamic solidarity" put into effect by King Faisal to fight against Gamal Abdel Nasser and his "progressive" allies, the kingdom at that time became a veritable religious melting pot where all those who were being persecuted for their Islamic activism could find refuge. Among those who found refuge were, first of all, a large number of members of the Muslim Brotherhood. The hybrid that took shape when the political and cultural aspects of their ideology encountered the religious concepts of Wahhabism is called al-Sahwa al-Islamiyya (the Islamic Awakening), shortened simply to the Sahwa. It is the politicized form of Salafism represented by the Sahwa, which is strongly anchored in the educational system, that has dominated the politico-religious sphere up to our time. Besides the Brotherhood, however, dozens of independent Islamic personalities, sometimes coming from a "Muslim Reformist" background, found refuge in Saudi Arabia at that time. Some of them, like Muhammad Nasir al-Din al-Albani, whose career we are about to trace, were to wield decisive influence over the future structure of the Saudi politico-religious sphere.

Al-Albani in Syria

Muhammad Nasir al-Din al-Albani was born in Albania in 1914 of a Hanafi *'alim* (religious scholar) father. In 1923, just after a secular takeover of the country on the heels of independence from the Ottoman Empire, his father decided to leave the country and settle with his family in Damascus. The young Nasir al-Din first learned Arabic and then the profession of watchmaker, while his father taught him the rudiments of religion in the purest tradition of Hanafi *fiqh*. His education might have stopped there had he not, from adolescence, been immoderately fond of reading. Thus, in his spare time, he spent many hours in the Maktaba Zahiriyya,[17] the first public library in Syria, founded in the early 1880s by one of the precursors of Muslim Reformism in the region, Tahir al-Jaza'iri.[18] In this way he became a self-taught expert on Islam, learning from books rather than from the *'ulama*. One of his biographers even states that al-Albani was distinguished in religious circles by how few *ijazat* (certificates)[19] he possessed.[20] As a result of his readings in the journal *al-Manar*, the major vehicle for the spread of Muslim Reformist ideas, and of his attendance[21] at the *majlis* of Muhammad Bahjat al-Bitar, a student of Jamal al-Din al-Qasimi, the father of Muslim Reformism in Syria, al-Albani, at the age of twenty, adhered to the Reformist tradition that was so fashionable among the "peripheral *'ulama*" of Damascus.[22] From this school he inherited his hostility to Sufism and popular Islam, and it was this that he theorized about early on, in his first work,[23] entitled *Tahdhir al-sajid min ittikhadh al-qubur masajid* [A warning to those who kneel down not to mistake tombs for mosques],[24] though, in his hands it took on more radical forms than it had in Muslim Reformism. From this source also came his refusal of *taqlid* (imitation); this he emphasized by rejecting the *madhahib* (the four canonical legal schools) themselves (to his father's extreme displeasure), and calling for a renewal of *ijtihad*. To enable this renewal, the Muslim Reformists—headed by Rashid Rida, the chief editor of *al-Manar*—had underlined the importance of a critical re-evaluation of the hadith, but without making this a central point of their doctrine.[25] They had in fact continued to let reason and independent opinion play a relatively important legal role; thus even their criticism of the hadith was intended to be both a "technical" review of the *sanad* (the hadith's chain of transmission) and a more "rational" critique of the *matn* (the content of the hadith).[26] Here al-Albani's approach differs radically from his teachers'; for al-Albani, who claims to follow, like the Indian Ahl-e Hadith, in the steps of the medieval school of the *ahl al-hadith*, the use of reason must, at all costs, be banned from the legal process.

To that end the hadith,[27] which provides answers (without calling on human reason) to problems with no solution in the Qur'an, must be placed at the heart of the process. Here al-Albani is once again greatly in tune with the Indian Ahl-e Hadith. He therefore sets the "science of hadith" (*'ilm al-hadith*) at the apex of the religious disciplines, eclipsing *fiqh*, which in his eyes is no longer anything more than a mere appendix, which he calls *fiqh al-hadith*, to it.[28] However, the science of hadith must itself be sheltered from reason; thus the critique of the *matn* must be strictly formal, i.e., linguistic or grammatical. Only the *sanad* may be truly called into question, and it is therefore by studying the *sanad* that the authenticity of a hadith can be determined. For al-Albani the most important discipline within the science of hadith becomes the "science of men" (*'ilm al-rijal*), which appraises the morality, and thereby the reliability of the transmitters; this discipline is also known as the "science of critical study and just appraisal" (*'ilm al-jarh wa-l-ta'dil*).

Another serious divergence from his reformist teachers is al-Albani's extension of the range of criticism to the whole corpus, which Rida, for example, had been reluctant to do, considering a hadith *mutawatir* (a hadith transmitted through multiple chains), handed down from generation to generation, to be beyond criticism.[29] Thus al-Albani did not hesitate to characterize as weak (*da'if*)[30] certain hadith taken from the two canonical collections of Bukhari and Muslim.

Al-Albani and Saudi Arabia

It was in the early 1950s that al-Albani became famous in Syria for his knowledge of hadith, which he taught weekly from 1954 in an informal circle (*majlis*).[31] In 1960 his popularity began to worry the government, who put him under surveillance even though he steered clear of taking any political stand.[32] He was therefore happy to accept the teaching post that the recently founded University of Medina offered him. His name was proposed by Shaykh 'Abd al-'Aziz b. Baz, the vice president of the university, who had close personal and intellectual ties to al-Albani. As emphasized above, Ibn Baz was strongly influenced in his student days by the teachings of Sa'd b. 'Atiq, who was converted to the ideas of the Ahl-e Hadith during his long stay in India, and he strongly shared al-Albani's interest in a renewal of hadith.[33] The battle was, nevertheless, far from being won; from the moment of his arrival, the presence of al-Albani stirred up sharp controversy within the Wahhabi community, which was still under the sway of unacknowledged partisans of the Hanbali *madhhab* (school of law), led by the mufti Muhammad b. Ibrahim Al al-Shaykh (1893–1969). For Al al-Shaykh, al-Albani's call for an *ijtihad* outside the framework of the established schools of law compromised the authority of the Wahhabi *'ulama*. But at the same time, the original paradox of Wahhabism, opposing a stated ideal of *ijtihad* to a legal practice stemming largely from the Hanbali school, made these *'ulama* particularly ill-armed to defend themselves on the intellectual level, and all the more so as al-Albani's creed (*'aqida*) was irreproachably Wahhabi. On several occasions fatwas handed down by al-Albani outraged the religious institution. The mufti, who refused to lower himself to reply to a person he still considered a young, second-tier *'alim*, delegated the task of refuting the Syrian shaykh to one of his chief assistants, Isma'il al-Ansari.[34] But al-Albani was growing ever more popular, and to get rid of him they had to wait until he committed a serious mistake. The opportunity arose when, after reassessing the authenticity of certain hadith accepted by the Hanbali school, al-Albani pleaded, in a work entitled *Hijab al-mar'a al-muslima* [The Muslim woman's veil], for women to be allowed not to cover their faces. Such a stand appeared unacceptable to Saudi religious groups of all persuasions. Thus, Muhammad b. Ibrahim had no trouble justifying the refusal to renew al-Albani's contract at the university, and forced him to leave the kingdom in 1963.[35] In May 1967, al-Albani was arrested in Syria and spent a month in prison before being freed, along with all other political prisoners in June.[36] This event probably motivated the offer he received the following year—under pressure from his protector Ibn Baz—to head the department of higher studies in the *shari'a* faculty in Mecca.[37] But the maneuver failed "due to the opposition of the authorities,"[38] thus demonstrating how keen the controversy surrounding al-Albani still remained. He was jailed again a few years later in Syria for eight months,[39] before leaving the country for Jordan in 1979.[40] As for Saudi Arabia, it finally granted him symbolic rehabilitation in 1975, making him a member of the High Council (al-Majlis al-A'la) of the Islamic University of Medina.[41] But even though al-Albani taught for only a relatively short time in Saudi Arabia—excluding his numerous invitations to conferences and his visits on the occasion of the pilgrimage—his ideas had a very strong impact there.[42] Overall, he encouraged a vast revival of interest in studying the hadith and its authenticity, and this affected all the religious currents. As an Islamist has explained, "The hadith had become a virtual dictatorship. When in a sermon or a conference an 'alim cited a hadith, he could be interrupted at any moment by one of his students asking him: 'Has that hadith been authenticated? Has al-Albani authenticated it?' That could hardly fail to reinforce the mistrust felt by the 'ulama belonging to the religious institution toward al-Albani."[43] It was through this same means that al-Albani, indirectly and perhaps despite his own wishes, exerted influence on the main Saudi Salafi movement, the Sahwa, for whom his calls to revive ijtihad were above all a way to legitimize political stands that diverged from the official line. Al-Albani, nevertheless, always played a relatively secondary role in the Sahwi corpus, and for good reason: those who made him their absolute reference are the Sahwa's sworn enemies.

From al-Albani to the Neo-Ahl al-Hadith

These self-proclaimed disciples of al-Albani took the name "Ahl al-Hadith," in reference to the medieval school from which he himself claimed to proceed. To distinguish them from their predecessors in the Middle Ages in this chapter we shall call them the "neo-Ahl al-Hadith." They adopt a stance that is critical both of the traditional Wahhabi religious institution and of the Sahwa, justifying this double opposition on certain of al-Albani's stands.

Al-Albani, as we have seen, denounced the Wahhabis' attachment to the Hanbali school, going so far as to say that Muhammad b. 'Abd al-Wahhab was Salafi in creed (*'aqida*), but not in law (*fiqh*). Moreover, in al-Albani's view Ibn 'Abd al-Wahhab did not know the hadith well, as is shown by the fact that one of his epistles contains a notoriously weak hadith.[44] Al-Albani thus plays here with the original inconsistency within Wahhabism, which we already pointed out, assigning himself not so much the role of Wahhabism's opponent as that of advocate for a regenerated Wahhabism purified of its elements, contrary to the doctrine of the pious predecessors. In taking up these ideas, the neo-Ahl al-Hadith are therefore attacking not the spirit of Wahhabism, which they claim to defend, but rather the legitimacy of the institution that has set itself up as the depository of that spirit. It should be pointed out, moreover, that this challenge to the legal methodology of Wahhabism in no way involves a broader criticism of its social positions—on the ban on photography, music, or tobacco, for instance—which the neo-Ahl al-Hadith mostly share. Al-Albani's opposition to the *niqab* (the veil that covers women's faces) should not give the impression that the neo-Ahl al-Hadith are much more socially liberal than the Wahhabis.

However, more than the Wahhabi religious establishment, with whom relations remained fairly cordial thanks to the presence of Ibn Baz, the neo-Ahl al-Hadith's main adversary was the Sahwa, outsiders like them in the Saudi religious field, but enjoying a strong tailwind since the early 1970s. As before, they would justify this opposition by referring to al-Albani and his stand on the Muslim Brotherhood—amalgamated by the neo-Ahl al-Hadith with the Sahwa—and to his position on political activism.

It should be recalled here that at a time when all the Islamic currents, even the Wahhabi religious community with Ibn Baz at the forefront,[45] paid homage to the "martyred" radical

Muslim Brotherhood ideologue Sayyid Qutb (executed in 1966 on Nasser's order), al-Albani was one of the first shaykhs to openly risk criticism of him. His main problem with Qutb was with his creed (*'aqida*), as set forth in his Qur'anic commentary, *Fi Zilal al-Qur'an* [*In the Shade of the Qur'an*]. In particular, al-Albani thought he detected in it signs of the loathed doctrine of the "unity of being" (*wahdat al-wujud*), defined by the Andalusian mystic Ibn 'Arabi (d. 1240) and assimilated with Sufism.[46] In addition, al-Albani took issue with Hasan al-Banna, the founder of the Muslim Brotherhood, denouncing his "stands contrary to the Sunna," and insisting on the fact that al-Banna was not a "religious scholar" (*'alim*).[47]

These attacks were directly linked to the other main fault for which he reproached the Brotherhood (and by extension their Sahwa emulators), i.e., being more interested in politics than in religious science (*'ilm*) and creed (*'aqida*). Al-Albani insisted, for his part, that his priorities were the opposite. Thus did he continue repeating this now famous sentence: "in the present circumstances, the good policy is to stay away from politics" (*min al-siyasa tark al-siyasa*).[48] Indeed, as he explained at a lecture delivered in Medina in 1977, through an indirect allusion to the Muslim Brotherhood:

> All Muslims agree on the need to establish an Islamic state, but they differ on the method to be employed to attain that goal. [For me] only by the Muslims' adhering to *tawhid* can the causes of their dissensions be removed, so that they may march toward their objective in closed ranks.[49]

It was in this spirit that he developed his theory of *da'wa* (preaching), which he calls *al-tasfiya wa-l-tarbiya* (purification and education) and explains as follows:

By *tasfiya* I mean the purification of Islam of everything
that is foreign to it and corrupts it. To that end the
Sunna must be purged of all the forged (*mawdu'*) and
weak (*da'if*) hadith that it contains, so that the Qur'an
may be interpreted in light of this authenticated Sunna
and the notions and concepts passed down from our
pious predecessors.[50]

As for the *tarbiya*, "it consists in instilling into our youth this
authentic Islamic creed (*'aqida*) drawn from the Qur'an and the
Sunna." The radical difference between this approach, which
places creed (*'aqida*) before politics and the individual before
the state, and the approach of the Muslim Brotherhood is
spectacularly illustrated by al-Albani's famous fatwa in which
he calls on the Palestinians to leave the occupied territories
of Gaza and the West Bank since they could, according to
him, no longer practice their religion correctly there. Given a
choice between protecting the creed (*'aqida*) and the land, he
adds, it is the creed that must receive priority.[51]

Al-Albani's stands were enshrined by the neo-Ahl al-
Hadith in a veritable ideological paradigm and engendered
a much more systematic argumentation against the Muslim
Brotherhood and by extension the Sahwa. Thence, in one of
his pamphlets deemed the most representative of this faction's
ideas, entitled *al-Makhraj min al-fitna* [How to escape from
internal dissension], dated 1982, the Yemeni shaykh, Muqbil
al-Wadi'i, who spent the 1970s at the Islamic University of
Medina and belonged to the group al-Jama'a al-Salafiyya al-
Muhtasiba (JSM), to which we shall be returning in detail a
bit further on, established a distinction between five "Islamic
groups": first, those he calls *ashab al-Hadith* (or Ahl al-Hadith),
whom he describes as "the group that God has designated to
preserve His religion"[52] and, identifying them with the early
traditionists (*muhaddithun*), as "those whose counsel is best

after the prophets and companions, for God, His messenger, His book, His leaders, and ordinary Muslims."[53] Second, in the middle, three groups to whom he addresses scathing criticism while still recognizing their virtues: the Egyptians of Ansar al-Sunna al-Muhammadiyya[54] (whom he reproaches for their lack of interest in the hadith, while singling out the importance of their calls for *tawhid*),[55] the Jama'at al-Takfir—the "*takfiris*"—whose enthusiasm and insistence on *dalil* (proof drawn from the sacred texts) he praises while lambasting their tendency to abuse the practice of *takfir* (excommunication),[56] and the Tabligh, praised for the efficacy of their teaching, but reproached for their neglect of *'aqida* and *'ilm* and for their attachment to the *madhhab*—in this case the Hanafi school. Finally, he addresses the Muslim Brotherhood for whom, after a brief introduction in which he underlines the initial good intentions of Hasan al-Banna, he directs his harshest and most virulent criticism. He blames them for not having *'ulama* in their ranks, for "forbidding their members to attend the *'ulama*'s classes," for simply "not liking [the *'ulama*]," for being consequently ignorant in the disciplines of religious knowledge,[57] and also for "preferring positions of power to the Sunna."[58]

At a moment when the Muslim Brotherhood was at the apex of its influence, al-Albani's stands—and the use to which they were put by his neo-Ahl al-Hadith disciples—caused a great deal of turmoil. They resulted, in the 1970s, in the Brotherhood's "boycotting [al-Albani's] lessons and everything connected with his *da'wa*" and publishing several attacks against him in its journal *al-Mujtama'*.[59]

This was an untenable position for someone who was already seeking to be recognized as one of the most highly respected religious authorities in the Muslim world. As a consequence, from the 1980s al-Albani tried ever harder to keep out of the disputes, even if that sometimes meant

45

having to disown his most enthusiastic disciples. This is why al-Albani, visibly surprised by the devastating effects of his stands on Sayyid Qutb, and probably fearing to alienate a whole sector of the Islamic sphere, sought to soften his statements by declaring:

> Yes, [Sayyid Qutb] must be refuted, but with composure, and dispassionately. . . Yes, he must be refuted, it is a duty. . . But that does not mean that we must show him hostility, or forget that he has certain merits. The important thing is that he is a Muslim and an Islamic writer—within the bounds of his own understanding of Islam, as I have already said—who was killed for the sake of *da'wa*, and that those who killed him are the enemies of God.[60]

However, such attempts proved to be useless; however hard al-Albani tried to appear as a consensual figure, it was already too late, as his disciples had already, partly despite his own wishes, set him up as the spiritual father of the neo-Ahl al-Hadith current.

Identity and Practices of the Neo-Ahl al-Hadith

Beyond this ideology, which conferred on the neo-Ahl al-Hadith a particular identity in the religious sphere, they also developed a number of practices that made them stand out in the social sphere. Most of these were grounded in some of al-Albani's fatwas that were in disagreement with the Hanbali–Wahhabi consensus. On the subject of prayer, for instance, the neo-Ahl al-Hadith tend to follow al-Albani's injunctions collected in a little book—which caused a great scandal when it came out—entitled *Sifat salat al-nabi* [The characteristics of the Prophet's prayer]. In it al-Albani advocates, for example, adding *"wa barakatuhu"* (and His blessings) to the ritual "*al-salam 'alaykum*," as well as holding one's hands during prayer in a way that significantly differs from the prescriptions of Hanbali–Wahhabi *fiqh*. Also, he approves of remaining shod while praying within the mosque. The conspicuous nature of these ritual differences explains why the emergence of the neo-Ahl al-Hadith aroused quarrels and arguments in the mosques of Medina and other cities where their movement had taken root, driving al-Albani's disciples to gather in mosques under their own control. These mosques have no *mihrab* (a niche oriented toward Mecca inside the mosque), as the neo-Ahl al-Hadith consider it a *bid'a* (a reprehensible innovation).[61] Insofar as their attire is concerned, the neo-Ahl al-Hadith, like the Sahwis but with even greater intransigence, stress the ban on wearing the *'iqal* (a circlet used to fasten the *shmagh* or the *ghutra*, the headcloths worn by the Saudis). As for the *thawb* (the Saudi robe), they demand that it should come up to half-calf ("four fingers under the knee"), mostly to distinguish themselves from the Sahwis, who wear it down to their ankles. As a former member of this group humorously puts it, "The aim is to show that the duty to present oneself humbly before God is stronger than the fear of ridicule."[62] Finally, some neo-Ahl al-Hadith tend to push imitation of the Prophet to the point of wearing their hair long, again setting them apart from the Sahwis, who feel that in the interest of *da'wa* one must be well-groomed.[63]

The Neo-Ahl al-Hadith's Early Bases in Saudi Arabia

It was in the 1960s that the neo-Ahl al-Hadith faction began to take shape at the Islamic University of Medina, and especially at Dar al-Hadith, a religious institute attached to the university. The history of this institute eloquently illustrates how the influence of the Indian Ahl-e Hadith prepared the way for the neo-Ahl al-Hadith. Dar al-Hadith was founded in 1931 by an Indian Ahl-e Hadith shaykh who was living in Medina, Ahmad b. Muhammad al-Dahlawi;[64] he was concerned with encouraging the study of hadith in the Hijaz and thereby disseminating the ideas of his movement there. At his death in 1955 the institute passed under the control of a Malian shaykh, a "traditional" specialist of hadith whose name was 'Abd al-Rahman al-Ifriqi, and then in 1957, after al-Ifriqi's demise, under shaykh 'Umar Falata[65] of West African origin. In 1964 the institute was attached to the Islamic University of Medina,[66] where it functioned as the de facto department of hadith until 1976, when such a department was officially set up.[67] In the 1960s al-Albani visited Dar al-Hadith frequently to give lectures, and some of his students, such as Ali al-Mazru', taught there. There were sharp disputes between al-Albani's disciples, already perceived as hadith revolutionaries, and the partisans of a more traditional concept of hadith study, like Hammad al-Ansari and 'Umar Falata, the institute's director.

In the 1970s, the influence of the al-Albani faction increased at the institute, a development that led, as we shall see, to the powerful rise of al-Jama'a al-Salafiyya al-Muhtasiba (JSM). Rapidly, however, al-Albani's influence reached the other main place where hadith was taught in the Hijaz, which had remained under the influence of the 'ulama who favored a more traditional approach. This was the Dar al-Hadith al-Khayriyya in Mecca, an institute founded in 1933 by 'Abd al-Zahir Abu al-Samh,[68] an Egyptian member of Ansar al-Sunna al-Muhammadiyya who had become imam of the Grand Mosque in Mecca a few years before.[69] From the 1970s onwards, the number of neo-Ahl al-Hadith there grew significantly. Finally, in Riyadh and in Burayda, there appeared small groups linked to the neo-Ahl al-Hadith, generally led by a charismatic individual, often the imam of a mosque.

Al-Albani's Heirs

Together with a sharp increase in the numbers of the neo-Ahl al-Hadith, the 1970s saw al-Albani's disciples split—despite their official claims of shunning politics—over the attitude to adopt toward the regime. Two main positions emerged during that period: the first, which advocates an active rejection of the state and its institutions, crystallized in the form of a "rejectionist" current, whose first manifestation was the storming of the Grand Mosque in Mecca in 1979 by a radicalized faction of al-Jama'a al-Salafiyya al-Muhtasiba. The second position, which is characterized by unconditional support for the ruler, first manifested itself in the wake of the Gulf War with the "Jami" current (in reference to Shaykh Muhammad Aman al-Jami, one of its leading figures).

Juhayman al-'Utaybi and the Rejectionists

Recent research[70] has shown that the group led by Juhayman al-'Utaybi, which occupied the Grand Mosque in Mecca for two weeks in November and December 1979, was a radicalized fraction of a larger pietistic movement, al-Jama'a al-Salafiyya al-Muhtasiba (JSM), literally, "the Salafi group that promotes virtue and prevents vice." The JSM was founded in Medina in the mid-1960s by disciples of al-Albani who were unhappy with the growing social influence of new religious actors such as the Muslim Brotherhood, the nascent Sahwa and the Tabligh. The JSM was characterized socially by its adhesion to most of the distinctive practices in attire and prayer preached by al-Albani. It was able to develop under the protection of 'Abd al-'Aziz b. Baz, who had become head of the Saudi religious establishment after the death of Mufti Muhammad b. Ibrahim in 1969, and had even agreed to be named the movement's supreme guide. Al-Albani often visited the JSM, mainly during the pilgrimage, giving lectures at Bayt al-Ikhwan, the headquarters of the movement located in a suburb of Medina.

49

One of the characteristic features of the JSM was its attitude toward politics and power; its members renounced any interest in politics, which they thought distracted the true believer from religious knowledge (*'ilm*) and from the rigor of creed (*'aqida*). As a consequence they—like al-Albani—made the Muslim Brotherhood the prime target of their criticism. Thus, when JSM members proclaim that the Saudi regime, like many other governments in the Muslim world, is illegitimate, they are not, *a priori*, proceeding from political motives, but rather on the simple principle that those wielding power do not come from the Prophet's tribe, Quraysh, the *sine qua non* condition for ruling the community stated by most of the classical jurists and taken up by al-Albani. Consequently, the oath of allegiance (*bay'a*) that links the Saudi regime to its subjects is, according to them, null and void (*batila*). This in no way means, however, that the individual members of the Saudi royal family should be excommunicated (*takfir*).

Nonetheless, for some of the JSM, drawn against their will toward the politicization they continued to reject formally, a number of precise grievances against the royal family, perceived as being too close to the West and to a large extent corrupt, were increasingly melded with this principle. This rising protest within the JSM contributed considerably to the rifts that tore it apart in 1977 and ended with a small hard core splitting off around Juhayman. Still, it should be noted that however radical they were, Juhayman and his companions never crossed the red line of *takfir* and continued to cling formally to the stands of JSM and al-Albani as to the attitude to take toward the regime. How then can the rise of these revolutionary urges within the radicalized fraction of the JSM be reconciled with a legal position that rejects using *takfir* against the rulers, without which it is illegitimate to oppose them with armed force? The solution was found,

if one dares to say so, in a divine intervention. At the end
of 1978 Juhayman announced to the members of his group
that the arrival of the Mahdi expected at the end of the
world to establish prosperity and justice over the earth,
was imminent, and a few months later that he was none
other than Muhammad al-Qahtani, a longtime companion
of Juhayman's in the JSM. For the prophecy to be fulfilled,
tradition ordains that the Mahdi has to be consecrated in the
heart of the Grand Mosque in Mecca between one of the
corners of the Ka'ba (al-rukn) and Abraham's prayer station
(al-maqam). The date chosen was the first day of the year of
the Hijra 1400, which corresponds to 20 November 1979. It
is therefore in this messianic line of reasoning that one must
seek the reasons behind the storming of the Grand Mosque
of Mecca—which had nothing to do with any clear political
strategy. The attack ended in fiasco, with Juhayman arrested
and later executed and his companions killed or arrested. Not
long after, al-Albani was accused of intellectual responsibility
for the creation of the JSM and so, indirectly, for the 1979
crisis. He was then forbidden to set foot in Saudi Arabia for
a number of years, but the ban was soon lifted, as it had been
previously, at the behest of Ibn Baz.

Al-Madkhali and the Jamis

The episode at the Grand Mosque of Mecca was a hard blow
for the rejectionist neo-Ahl al-Hadith and led, within the
wider neo-Ahl al-Hadith movement, as if in compensation,
to an ostentatiously exacerbated frenzy of loyalism toward
the Saudi royal family. This gave rise in the 1980s to a
loyalist neo-Ahl al-Hadith faction, under the banner of two
illustrious individuals, Shaykh Muhammad Aman al-Jami,
from whose name this current came to be known as Jami,
and Shaykh Rabi' al-Madkhali, both of them professors of
hadith at the Islamic University of Medina. In doctrine the

Jamis largely continue to follow the injunctions of al-Albani, questioning only his principle of denying the legitimacy of a non-Qurayshi ruler, as the Saudi state is, in their eyes, a pure Islamic state.

While they were relatively marginal at the end of the 1980s, they found themselves thrust to the forefront by the Gulf War. King Fahd's appeal to the American troops to protect the kingdom five days after the Iraqi invasion of Kuwait on 2 August 1990 stirred up quite of bit of turmoil in Saudi Arabia. It was after this event that the Sahwa, acting here as proponent of a politicized version of Salafism, took the reins of an uncompromising Islamist opposition aimed against the Saudi regime, of which it demanded both the departure of the Americans and a substantial reform of the political system. Against this wave of protest, the Jamis, who had gained considerable experience in attacking the Muslim Brotherhood and the Sahwa since the 1960s, appeared to the regime as first-rate allies. In no time they were granted considerable resources to lead a major counter-offensive against the Islamist opposition. Al-Jami, al-Madkhali and others were offered official tribunes for their sermons, in which they put to good use the well-tried rhetoric of the neo-Ahl al-Hadith against their Sahwi adversaries. They claimed that Sahwi opposition to the Saudi regime was nothing but a predictable consequence of the Sahwis' indifference toward genuine 'ilm and of their opportunism. Thus did the Jamis counter the Sahwa's politicized Salafism with an assertive and militant apolitical stance, complemented by unconditional loyalism toward the royal family.[71]

The Exportation of the Neo–Ahl al-Hadith
Even though the dynamics that initially gave birth to the neo-Ahl al-Hadith must be understood within the Saudi context, the movement was rapidly exported out of Arabia, so that

today it constitutes an unavoidable element of Salafi Islam in many Muslim and Western countries. The vehicles of its exportation were of two kinds.

The first kind of vehicle was personal. It was above all Nasir al-Din al-Albani himself who, in every country where he stayed, trained students who endeavored to perpetuate his teaching, as in Syria, where he resided until 1979, and Jordan, where he emigrated afterwards and settled until his death. The leeway he enjoyed in the Hashemite kingdom partly explains the strong implantation of the neo-Ahl al-Hadith community in that country.[72] Another sizable conveyor of the neo-Ahl al-Hadith doctrine was the Yemeni Muqbil al-Wadi'i, one of al-Albani's students and a member of the JSM in the 1970s before his expulsion in 1978 to his native Yemen, where he emerged locally as the founding father of Salafism. The social and religious clout acquired by al-Wadi'i in Yemen explains the central role played by the neo-Ahl al-Hadith in the makeup of Yemeni Salafism.

The second type of vehicle for the export of Salafism was institutional. While the neo-Ahl al-Hadith filled a relatively small slot up to the end of the 1980s in the Islamic institutions of the kingdom, the rise of Jamism in 1991–92 was such that its proponents were granted control of several of those institutions, certain of which were linked to the export of Saudi Islam. The most important of these institutions was the Islamic University of Medina, taken over by al-Jami and al-Madkhali, who managed to get most of the Muslim Brotherhood and Sahwis who taught there dismissed. The stakes were high; a large majority of the university's students are foreigners, destined to go home to their countries once their education is completed. Therefore, transforming it into a Jami stronghold from 1992–93 had a strong impact on the nature of the Salafism that was thereafter exported from Saudi Arabia. The fact that Salafism was implanted in France in large part by graduates of this university, such as Imam Abdelkader Bouziane (expelled to Algeria in 2004),[73] who had come back from Medina in the mid-1990s, goes a long way to explain why Jamism, and to a greater extent the neo-Ahl al-Hadith current of thought, hold such a preponderantly dominant position within Salafi Islam in France.

Conclusion: The Neo-Ahl al-Hadith Today

Through the originality of his legal positions and his dogged opposition to the growing influence of the Muslim Brotherhood and the Sahwa in the Saudi religious sphere and beyond, Nasir al-Din al-Albani provided the doctrinal corpus necessary for the emergence of a powerful neo-Ahl al-Hadith current, infused with the desire to regenerate Wahhabism while simultaneously stressing a militant stand against any involvement in politics. This current is today dominant within Salafism in several countries, such as France and Yemen. It is strongly present in other countries—such as Saudi Arabia, Jordan, Kuwait, and Algeria—whose regimes have long understood how useful it could be to counterbalance the rise of a politicized form of Salafism that poses an often unprecedented challenge to their authority. For this very reason, in the post-9/11 world, these regimes see it as more indispensable than ever. This is, in part, why it will continue, in the years to come, to represent one of the main components of Salafi Islam.

1 There are several reasons why we have used Juhayman and not al-'Utaybi on second reference. First is convention—most academic articles we have seen use his first name. The convention itself stems from the fact that most Saudis refer to him by his first name. This is partly because Juhayman is an uncommon name, whereas al-'Utaybi is very common.

2 For a reliable and updated account of the siege, see Lawrence Wright, *The Looming Tower: Al-Qaeda and the Road to 9/11* (New York: Knopf, 2006), 88–94.

3 The main works on the history of Saudi Arabia mention Juhayman only in very brief terms; see, for example, Alexei Vassiliev, *The History of Saudi Arabia* (London: Saqi, 2000), 395–97; Madawi al-Rasheed, *A History of Saudi Arabia* (Cambridge: Cambridge University Press, 2002), 144–46. A few English-language academic books and articles have dealt with the phenomenon in somewhat more detail, but most of them are based on secondary sources in Arabic; see James Buchan, "The Return of the Ikhwan-1979," in David Holden and Richard Johns, *The House of Saud: The Rise and Rule of the Most Powerful Dynasty in the Arab World* (New York: Holt, Rinehart and Winston, 1981), 511–26; Ayman al-Yassini, *Religion and State in the Kingdom of Saudi Arabia* (Boulder, CO: Westview, 1985), 124–27; R. Hrair Dekmejian, *Islam in Revolution: Fundamentalism in the Arab World* (Syracuse, NY: Syracuse University Press, 1985), 133–7; Nazih Ayubi, *Political Islam* (London: Routledge, 1994), 99–104; Joshua Teitelbaum, *Holier than Thou: Saudi Arabia's Islamic Opposition* (Washington, D.C.: Washington Institute for Near East Policy,

2000), 19–21. Perhaps the only Western study to make systematic use of primary sources is Joseph Kechichian's excellent 1990 article on Juhayman's letters; see Joseph A. Kechichian, "Islamic Revivalism and Change in Saudi Arabia: Juhayman al-'Utaybi's 'Letters to the Saudi People,'" *Muslim World* 70 (1990), 1–16; see also Kechichian, "The Role of the Ulama in the Politics of an Islamic State: The Case of Saudi Arabia," *International Journal of Middle East Studies* 18 (1986), 53–71.

4 Perhaps the most well-known work is that of Rifat Sayyid Ahmad entitled *Rasa'il Juhayman al-'Utaybi, qa'id al-muqtahimin li-l-Masjid al-Haram bi-Makka* [The letters of Juhayman al-'Utaybi, leader of the invaders of the sacred mosque in Mecca] (Cairo: Madbuli, 2004). A Saudi leftist militant has produced a long and interesting work under the pseudonym Abu Dharr; see Abu Dharr, *Thawra fi rihab Makka* [Revolution in the Mecca precinct] (Kuwait: Dar Sawt al-Tali'a, 1980). The text was first published in the leftist opposition magazine *Sawt al-tali'a*, 21 April 1980, under the name "Ahdath al-Haram bayna al-haqa'iq wa-l-abatil" [The haram events, between truth and lies]. The London-based Saudi Shi'ite opposition has produced several interesting works: *Intifadat al-haram* [Uprising in the sanctuary] (London: Munazzamat al-Thawra al-Islamiyya fi al-Jazira al-Arabiyya, 1981), which the organization first published in its magazine before publishing it as a book; as well as *Zilzal Juhayman fi Makka* [Juhayman's earthquake in Mecca] (n.p., 1986), signed by a certain Fahd al-Qahtani, a pseudonym for Hamza al-Hasan, a Shi'ite opposition figure based in London. Another work is 'Abd al-'Azim al-Mat'ani, *Jarimat al-'asr: Qissat ihtilal al-Masjid al-Haram: riwayat shahid 'iyan* [The crime of the age: Eyewitness account of the occupation of the sacred mosque] (Cairo: Dar al-Ansar, 1980).

5 See *al-Riyadh*: 10 June 2003, 18 June 2003, 9 May 2004, 6 September 2004. See also articles by Mishari al-Dhayidi in *al-Sharq al-awsat*, 24 and 25 February 2004; and Adil al-Turayfi in *al-Riyadh*, 10 and 13 March 2004.

6 Stéphane Lacroix, "Saudi Arabia's Islamo-Liberal Reformists," *Middle East Journal* 58 (2004), 345–65.

7 This inquiry revealed, for example, that Hamza al-Hasan based *Zilzal Juhayman fi Makka* on interviews with two former members of the JSM other than al-Huzaymi. Another finding is that Abu Dharr (author of *Thawra fi rihab Makka*) is not the pseudonym of an Islamist commentator as previously believed (Kechichian, "Islamic Revivalism," 12), but an old nom de guerre of a leftist activist linked to the Saudi Ba'th party. According to Hamza al-Hasan, Abu Dharr's insights stem from the fact that he was based in Iraq and had access to Iraqi intelligence sources; interview with Hamza al-Hasan, London, February 2006.

8 Salafism (along with Wahhabism) is defined in chapter 2.

9 In this book, "Islamism" is understood in a very broad sense as "Islamic activism" directed at either the state or society.

10 See Stéphane Lacroix and Thomas Hegghammer, *Saudi Arabia Backgrounder: Who Are the Islamists?* (Brussels: International Crisis Group, 2004).

11 Vasiliev, *The History of Saudi Arabia*, 272.

12 Lacroix and Hegghammer, *Saudi Arabia Backgrounder*.

13 'Abd al-'Aziz b. Baz (1909–99), grand mufti of Saudi Arabia from 1993 until his death in 1999, became one of the most respected figures of the Wahhabi religious establishment in the late twentieth century.

14 The founding members included Sulayman al-Shtawi and Sa'd al-Tamimi. Interviews with Nasir al-Huzaymi, Riyadh, April 2004 and April 2005.

15 The Jama'at al-Tabligh (usually known as Tabligh or Tablighi Jama'at) is a pietistic and apolitical missionary organization founded in India in the late nineteenth century. Although it was quite popular among Saudi youth in the 1970s, the senior shaykhs of the religious establishment reproached it for not subscribing entirely to the Wahhabi creed (they regarded the Tablighis as "Sufis").

16 Abu Bakr al-Jaza'iri (literally "the Algerian") was born in 1921 in south Algeria, where he frequented religious circles close to Shaykh 'Abd al-Hamid b. Badis, before leaving the country in 1952

to settle in Saudi Arabia. He worked as a professor at the Islamic University of Medina from its foundation in 1961 until his retirement in 1986. He is known in Salafi circles to have been close to the Tabligh, which could explain the interest he found in a grassroots proselytizing and pietistic movement such as the JSM. For his biography, see Muhammad al-Majdhub, *'Ulama' wa mufakkirun 'araftuhum—al-juz' al-awwal* [Scholars and thinkers I have known—vol. one] (Cairo: Dar al-I'tisam, 1986).

17 Interview with Saudi Islamist, Riyadh, November 2005.

18 Al-Huzaymi says that there were in fact two separate episodes referred to by JSM members as "the breaking of the pictures." The second incident occurred in the mid-1970s, when JSM members were arrested for breaking pictures of the newly crowned King Khalid.

19 Ibn Baz's position on this matter can probably be explained by mainstream Salafism's traditionally negative attitude toward the creation of parties, organizations, or groups, which are considered as fragmenting the community, and, therefore, as a means for sedition (*fitna*). The only exception is the groups of *mutawwa'un* (often described as Saudi Arabia's religious police), who are seen as putting into practice the Qur'anic injunction of *al-amr bi-l-maruf wa-l-nahi 'an al-munkar* (commanding right and forbidding wrong), a function also called *hisba*; see Michael Cook, *Commanding Right and Forbidding Wrong in Islamic Thought* (Cambridge: Cambridge University Press, 2001).

20 It must be emphasized here that the JSM emerged as a perfectly legal pietistic movement which, according to al-Huzaymi, actually produced documents with its name printed on the letterhead. Ibn Baz's involvement should, therefore, not be interpreted as an unholy alliance with a clandestine Islamist opposition group.

21 See *al-Riyadh*, 9 May 2004.

22 Al-Huzaymi, interview.

23 Al-Huzaymi's information is unique because until recently the only available source on the rebels' profiles was the list of names

and nationalities of the sixty-three rebels executed in January 1980, published in the Saudi press at the time. This list has two significant limitations: first, it does not allow us to distinguish between a *badawi* and a *qabali*, nor between foreigners with and without Saudi citizenship. Second, the list is likely to include individuals who joined the rebels immediately before the attack and who were not necessarily longtime followers of Juhayman. In contrast, al-Huzaymi was able to provide us with substantial information on the background of individuals whom he personally met during his time as a JSM member in Medina, or as a prisoner.

24 The term *badawi* (pl. *badu*) usually refers to members of bedouin tribes who "recently" became sedentary, in most cases at the time of the 1920s Ikhwan and after. A *badawi* is distinguished from a *qabali* (tribal) person, who is basically a *hadari* (sedentary) person with a tribal genealogy. Among the *hadar* (sedentary people), the *qabali* is himself distinguished from the *khadiri*, who has no tribal genealogy.

25 Of thirty-five individuals, we have fifteen *badu* in total (i.e., 43 percent), five Harbi, five Shammari, three 'Utaybi, one Tamimi, and one unknown. The relatively high number of individuals from Harb and Shammar compared to that of 'Utayba should not surprise the reader, as al-Huzaymi was mainly based in Medina, which is closer to these two tribes' territory. The presence of these individuals also proves that the 'Utayba was only one of many *badu* elements in Juhayman's Ikhwan.

26 Steffen Hertog, "Segmented Clientelism: The Politics of Economic Reform in Saudi Arabia" (PhD diss., Oxford University, 2006).

27 Nine (i.e., almost 25 percent) of the thirty-five people described by al-Huzaymi were of foreign origin. Six had a Yemeni background, and one was from the Saudi–Yemeni border region of Najran. Al-Huzaymi's sample also includes a Saudi of Egyptian origin and a Saudi of Iranian origin. The Yemenis in particular featured prominently in the movement. Muqbil al-Wadi'i was considered one of their main scholars, Ahmad al-Mu'allim

administered Bayt al-Ikhwan, and Yusuf Bajunayd was a key financial contributor.

28 In Saudi Arabia, the relationship between social background on the one hand and socioeconomic status on the other is a complex one. Individuals of foreign descent may be socially and politically marginalized but are not necessarily economically disadvantaged. (Yusuf Bajunayd, a wealthy Saudi of Yemeni origin who funded Juhayman's group, is a case in point.) Conversely, *badu* may enjoy a high social status but remain economically weak.

29 Al-Yassini, *Religion and State*, 125.

30 Al-Huzaymi recalls his visit to a tent camp in Mina outside Mecca during the hajj in early December 1976. The tent housed around 250 people, most of whom were JSM members. Al-Albani and Juhayman were in close contact. Al-Albani held many lectures over consecutive days.

31 The Ahl-e Hadith is an Islamic revivalist movement founded in Bhopal, India, in the mid-nineteenth century. It puts great emphasis on the study of hadith and rejects all schools of jurisprudence. Ansar al-Sunna al-Muhammadiyya was founded in Egypt in 1926 by Muhammad Hamid al-Fiqqi, a Salafi scholar heavily influenced by the teachings of Ibn Taymiyya. Both Ahl-e Hadith and Ansar al-Sunna al-Muhammadiyya have maintained strong links to Saudi Arabia and the Wahhabi religious establishment throughout the twentieth century.

32 Muqbil al-Wadi'i writes that, although they did follow many of al-Albani's views, they also differed with him on a small number of issues; see Muqbil al-Wadi'i, *al-Makhraj min al-fitna* (Sanaa: Maktabat San'a al-Athariyya, 2002), 140.

33 Al-Wadi'i, *al-Makhraj min al-fitna*, 140.

34 The details and significance of the rooftop meeting have been confirmed and corroborated by several independent sources; al-Wadi'i, *al-Makhraj min al-fitna*; al-Huzaymi, interview; and Nabil Mouline's interview (in Mecca in April 2005) with a senior Wahhabi shaykh who attended the meeting.

35 Al-Wadiʻi, *al-Makhraj min al-fitna*, 141.

36 *Al-Sharq al-awsat*, 24 and 25 February 2004.

37 Al-Huzaymi, interview. See also *al-Sharq al-awsat*, 24 and 25 February 2004.

38 Kechichian, "Islamic Revivalism and Change in Saudi Arabia," 11.

39 *Intifadat al-Haram*, 35–39.

40 Al-Huzaymi, interview.

41 *Al-Riyadh*, 18 June 2003.

42 After failing to get the JSM to renounce their controversial practices, the senior scholars alerted the authorities and allegedly started falsely accusing the JSM of possessing weapons and preparing a coup; al-Huzaymi, interview; al-Wadiʻi, *al-Makhraj min al-fitna*, 141.

43 Al-Huzaymi, interview.

44 In Riyadh, for example, four or five people were arrested, including Muhammad al-Qahtani (the future Mahdi) and Muhammad al-Haydari (head of the JSM Riyadh branch).

45 Al-Huzaymi recalls a general meeting for the remaining members, held in the desert along the Qasim road between Riyadh and Sudayr a few weeks after the first arrests. According to al-Huzaymi, the meeting was attended by approximately eighty people.

46 Tape recordings of Juhayman were circulating in Islamist circles in Saudi Arabia at least as late as the early 1990s.

47 Kechichian, "Islamic Revivalism and Change in Saudi Arabia."

48 According to Muslim tradition, the Mahdi is a figure who appears towards the end of time. He restores justice in a time of corruption and religious deterioration. His appearance heralds the coming of the Messiah (*al-masih*).

49 Al-Huzaymi, interview.

50 Juhayman himself claimed that Ibn Baz had found "nothing

wrong in it." See "Da'wat al-ikhwan" [The call of the Ikhwan], quoted by al-Qahtani, *Zilzal Juhayman fi Makka*, 28.

51 Al-Huzaymi, interview. He took part personally in the distribution.

52 The first letter was entitled "Raf' al-iltibas 'an millat man ja'alahu Allah imaman li-l-nas" [Clarification about the community of whom God has made a guide for the people]; the group of seven pamphlets was entitled "al-Rasa'il al-sab'" [The seven letters]. The group of four bore the title "Majmu'at rasa'il al-imara wa-l-tawhid wa-da'wat al-ikhwan wa-l-mizan li-hayat al-insan" [Group of the letters: 'The state,' 'The unity of God,' 'The call of the brotherhood,' and 'The scale for the life of man']; Abu Dharr, *Thawra fi rihab Makka*, 113.

53 "Da'wat al-ikhwan," quoted in al-Qahtani, *Zilzal Juhayman fi Makka*, 37.

54 Muqbil al-Wadi'i, *Tarjamat Abi 'Abd al-Rahman Muqbil b. Hadi al-Wadi'i* (Sanaa: Dar al-Athar, 2002), 27.

55 Telephone interview with 'Abd al-Rahman 'Abd al-Khaliq in Khalid Sultan's office, Kuwait, May 2005. Some of these early refutations have later been collected in a book by 'Abd al-Khaliq entitled *al-Wala' wa-l-bara'* [Loyalty and dissociation].

56 Interviews with Khalid Sultan and Isma'il al-Shatti, Kuwait, May 2005.

57 Their writings were compiled in the early twentieth century in an influential book known as *al-Durar al-saniyya fi-l-ajwiba al-Najdiyya* [The glittering pearls of the Najdi answers].

58 "Al-Fitan wa akhbar al-Mahdi wa nuzul 'Isa 'alayhi al-salam wa ashrat al-sa'a" [Turmoil and the reports of the Mahdi and the coming of Jesus—peace be upon him—and the portents of the last hour].

59 Ahmad, *Rasa'il Juhayman al-'Utaybi,* 209.

60 According to al-Huzaymi, al-Qahtani had been imam at the small al-Ruwayl mosque in Riyadh, and was one of the founding

members of the JSM's Riyadh branch.

61 Muhammad al-Qahtani claimed that his ancestor, a *sharif* (pl. *ashraf*), had come from Egypt with Muhammad 'Ali's army in the early nineteenth century and had settled in one the villages inhabited by the members of the tribe of Qahtan, therefore, becoming a "Qahtani by alliance."

62 "The Mahdi will be of my stock, and will have a broad forehead and a prominent nose." *Sunan Abu Dawud*, 36, 4272.

63 "Disagreement will occur at the death of a caliph and a man of the people of Medina will come flying forth to Mecca. Some of the people of Mecca will come to him, bring him out against his will and swear allegiance to him between the *rukn* and the *maqam*. An expeditionary force will then be sent against him from Syria but will be swallowed up in the desert between Mecca and Medina. When the people see that, the eminent saints of Syria and the best people of Iraq will come to him and swear allegiance to him between the *rukn* and the *maqam*." *Sunan Abu Dawud*, 36, 4273.

64 See, for example, Ella Landau-Tasseron, "The Cyclical Reform: A Study of the *mujaddid* Tradition," *Studia Islamica* 70 (1989).

65 The authors thank Professor Berhard Haykel for this analysis.

66 Toby Craig Jones, "Rebellion on the Saudi Periphery, Modernity, Marginalization and the Shia Uprising of 1979," *International Journal of Middle East Studies* 38 (2006), 213–33.

67 A British journalist stationed in Saudi Arabia at the time says he interviewed a Saudi farmer in December 1979 who said he had observed a group of ragged men firing weapons in a field outside Mecca in November 1979; Interview with James Buchan, London, February 2006.

68 Al-Huzaymi, interview.

69 Abu Dharr, *Thawra fi rihab Mecca*, 125.

70 *Al-Sharq al-awsat*, 6 April 2005.

71 Among the prominent Kuwaiti JSM members at the time were Jabir al-Jalahma, who subsequently became a prominent jihadist

figure; 'Abdallah al-Nafisi, one of the most influential Islamist thinkers in Kuwait; and Khalid al-'Adwa, who later joined the mainstream Salafi current and became a member of parliament.

72 *Al-Riyadh*, 19 and 26 May 2003; Gilles Kepel, *Muslim Extremism in Egypt* (Berkeley: University of California Press, 2003), 89.

73 Al-Huzaymi, interview; al-Wadi'i, *al-Makhraj min al-fitna,* 141.

74 See, for instance, Ahmad, *Rasa'il Juhayman al-'Utaybi*, 62–63.

75 Ibid, 84.

76 A separate incident narrated by al-Huzaymi illustrates this sense of loyalty. When 'Abdallah al-Harbi, a former JSM member who did not believe in the Mahdi and had left the group, heard the news of the storming of the Grand Mosque, he decided to organize the storming of the Medina mosque to diminish the pressure on Juhayman and his followers. However, he was shot by police at a checkpoint on his way to Sajir to gather followers for his project.

77 One possible explanation for these declarations is that the Saudi leftist opposition tried to take advantage of the political situation to regain the visibility it had lost since the late 1960s.

78 Nasir al-Sa'id in al-Dustur, quoted in *MERIP Report* 85 (1980), 17.

79 Abu Muhammad al-Maqdisi, for instance, writes that he received confirmation from former JSM members that there was no broader plan, and no operations in other cities. See Abu Muhammad al-Maqdisi, "al-Kawashif al-jaliyya fi kufr al-dawla al-Sa'udiyya" [The obvious proofs of the Saudi state's impiety], 197, available at www.tawhed.ws.

80 See al-Maqdisi's 1998 interview with the Islamist magazine *Nida' al-Islam*, available at www.tawhed.ws.

81 Al-Maqdisi later married the sister of al-Dirbas' wife. See *al-Sharq al-awsat*, 15 May and 7 July 2003.

82 See in particular "Millat Ibrahim" [Abraham's Creed] from 1984 (available at www.tawhed.ws), in which he adopts and further develops Juhayman's doctrinal system, and "I'dad al-qada al-fawaris

bi-hajr fasad al-madaris" [Preparing shrewd leaders by abandoning the corruption of the schools] from 1989 (available at www.tawhed. ws), in which al-Maqdisi reiterates Juhayman's rejection of state education and employment.

83 Al-Maqdisi, "al-Kawashif al-jaliyya," 198.

84 Interview with 'Abdallah al-'Utaybi, Riyadh, April 2004.

85 Interview with Mishari al-Dhayidi, Jedda, June 2003. Interviews with 'Abdallah al-'Utaybi and unidentified Saudi former Islamist, Riyadh, April 2004.

86 The leadership core included Mishari al-Dhayidi and 'Abdallah al-'Utaybi. They have subsequently become outspoken liberals and prominent writers.

87 Bayt Shubra residents were primarily in contact with bedouins in northwestern Najd, whom they accessed through a Pakistani former member of JSM who lived in the town of al-Rass. Interview with Saud al-Sarhan, Riyadh, April 2004.

88 Interview with unidentified Saudi former Islamist.

89 Ibrahim al-Rayyis and Saud al-'Utaybi frequented Bayt Shubra regularly. 'Abd al-'Aziz al-Muqrin visited once or twice. Interview with al-'Utaybi. See also *al-Sharq al-awsat*, 9 December 2003 and 6 April 2005.

90 Just outside the city of Burayda, a community known as the "*ikhwan* of Burayda" (brotherhood of Burayda) lives in near isolation from the society around them. They do not interact with the state and refuse to adopt modern technologies such as electricity, cars, or telephones. There were similarities and even direct links between the JSM and the *ikhwan* of Burayda. Another ultraconservative and isolationist community is found in the neighborhood called *hayy al-muhajirin* in the Najdi city of Zulfi.

1 Traditionists are *'ulama* specialized in hadith.

2 According to a saying attributed to shaykh 'Abd al-'Aziz b. Baz.

3 Henri Laoust, "Le réformisme orthodoxe des 'salafiya' et les caractères généraux de son orientation actuelle," in Henri Laoust, *Pluralismes dans l'Islam* (Paris: Geuthner, 1983), 182.

4 This refers to the righteous Muslims of the first three centuries of Islam.

5 For more on doctrine, see Roel Meijer, ed., "Introduction," in *Global Salafism: Islam's New Religious Movement* (London: Hurst and Company, 2009), and Bernard Haykel, "On the Nature of Salafi Thought and Action," ibid., 33–57.

6 On Ibn 'Abd al-Wahhab's doctrine, see David Commins, *The Wahhabi Mission and Saudi Arabia* (London: I.B. Tauris, 2006), and 'Abd al-'Aziz al-Fahad, "From Exclusivism to Accommodation: Doctrinal and Legal Evolution of Wahhabism," *New York University Law Review* 79, no. 2 (May 2004), 485–519.

7 The term *fiqh* is sometimes translated as "jurisprudence." However, because al-Albani's doctrine precisely rejects the principle of jurisprudence, it is better translated here as "law."

8 Commins, *Wahhabi Mission*, 12.

9 The Sunna designates the Prophet's tradition, as transmitted through the hadith.

10 *al-Rasa'il al-shakhsiyya li-l-shaykh Muhammad b. 'Abd al-Wahhab* [The personal letters of shaykh Muhammad b. 'Abd al-Wahhab] (N.p.: n.d.), 39.

11 Frank E. Vogel, *Islamic Law and Legal System: Studies of Saudi Arabia* (Leiden: Brill, 2000), 74–76.

12 Barbara Metcalf, *Islamic Revival in British India: Deoband, 1860–1900* (Princeton, NJ: Princeton University Press, 1982), 270–78.

13 Commins, *Wahhabi Mission*, 145.

14 For this reason, the Ahl-e Hadith are sometimes dubbed "Wahhabis" in India.

15 Metcalf, *Islamic Revival*, 275–77.

16 'Abdallah al-Bassam, *'Ulama Najd khilal thamaniyat qurun* [The Wahhabi ulama across eight centuries] (Riyadh: Dar al-'Asima, 1398), 223.

17 Ibrahim Muhammad al-'Ali, *Muhammad Nasir al-Din al-Albani—muhaddith al-'asr wa nasir al-Sunna* [Muhammad Nasir al-Din al-Albani—Traditionist of the era and champion of the Sunna] (Damascus: Dar al-Qal'a, 2001), 11–17.

18 David Commins, *Islamic Reform: Politics and Social Change in Late Ottoman Syria* (New York: Oxford University Press, 1990), 42.

19 An *ijaza* is a certificate delivered by a religious scholar to a student of his whom he considers able to transmit part or all of his teachings.

20 'Abdallah b. Muhammad al-Shamrani, *Thabatu mu'allafat al-muhaddith al-kabir al-imam Muhammad Nasir al-Din al-Albani* [Index of the writings of the great traditionist Imam Muhammad Nasir al-Din al-Albani], www.dorar.net, 17; accessed 2 January 2011.

21 *Nubdha mukhtasara 'an al-sira al-dhatiyya li-fadhilat al-shaykh Muhammad Nasir al-Din b. al-Hajj Nuh al-Albani rahamahu Allah* [Short abstract of the biography of the venerable Shaykh Muhammad Nasir al-Din b. Nuh al-Albani, may God have mercy upon him], http://saaid.net/Warathah/1/albani.htm; accessed 2 January 2011.

22 See Commins, *Islamic Reform*. For the term "peripheral ulama," see Malika Zeghal, *Gardiens de l'Islam* (Paris: Presses de Sciences Po, 1996), 21.

23 al-Shamrani, *Thabatu mu'allafat al-muhaddith al-kabir*, 40.

24 Muhammad al-Majdhub, *'Ulama' wa mufakkirun 'araftuhum*, 290.

25 Daniel Brown, *Rethinking Tradition in Modern Islamic Thought* (Cambridge: Cambridge University Press, 2003), 40–41.

26 Ibid., 113–17.

27 al-Majdhub, *'Ulama' wa mufakkirun 'araftuhum*, 291.

28 al-Shamrani, *Thabatu mu'allafat al-muhaddith al-kabir*, 109–10.

29 Brown, *Rethinking Tradition in Modern Islamic Thought*, 41.

30 A hadith is said to be "weak" (*da'if*) when there are strong reasons to doubt its authenticity.

31 al-'Ali, *Muhammad Nasir al-Din al-Albani*, 30.

32 Biographical elements about Nasir al-Din al-Albani, http://www.islamway.com/bindex.php?section=scholarinfo&scholar_id=47; accessed 2 January 2011.

33 Interview with Sa'ud al-Sarhan, Riyadh, April 2005.

34 The first refutation is called "Ibahat al-tahalli bi-l-dhahab al-muhallaqli-l-nisa' wa al-radd 'ala al-Albani fi tahrimihi" [Authorizing women to wear golden rings or bracelets and refuting al-Albani's prohibition]. See al-Shamrani, *Thabatu mu'allafat al-muhaddith al-kabir*, 161. The second refutation, which came as a reaction to al-Albani's claims that Ibn 'Abd al-Wahhab was ignorant in hadith, is entitled "al-Intisar li-shaykh al-Islam Muhammad b. 'Abd al-Wahhab bi-l-radd 'ala mujanabat al-Albani li-l-sawab" [Defending the shaykh of Islam Muhammad b. 'Abd al-Wahhab by refuting al-Albani's errors], see al-Shamrani, *Thabatu mu'allafat al-muhaddith al-kabir*, 164. Al-Shamrani's list contains the titles of three other refutations on 165–76.

35 Interview with a former disciple of al-Albani, Riyadh, December 2005.

36 http://www.islamway.com/bindexphp?section=scholarinfo&scholar_id=47.

37 al-'Ali, *Muhammad Nasir al-Din al-Albani*, 31.

38 Muhammad Surur Zayn al-'Abidin, "Shaykh muhaddithi al-'asr fi dhimmat allah" [The shaykh of the traditionalists of the

age under the protection of God] *Majallat al-sunna* 90 (Rajab 1420 [October 1999]).

39 http://www.islamway.com/bindexphp?section=scholarinfo&s cholar_id=47; accessed 2 January 2011.

40 Quintan Wiktorowicz, *The Management of Islamic Activism: Salafis, the Muslim Brotherhood, and State Power in Jordan* (Albany: State University of New York Press, 2001), 120.

41 al-'Ali, *Muhammad Nasir al-Din al-Albani*, 31.

42 This explains why Frank Vogel noted that in the 1980s "Saudi ulama seem more disposed to claim *mujtahid* status than were their Wahhabi forefathers. Today, one can notice reticence to admit any school affiliation at all." See Vogel, *Islamic Law and Legal System*, 78.

43 Interview with a former member of the neo-Ahl al-Hadith, Jedda, April 2005.

44 Recordings are available at: http://www.albrhan.org/fetan/b1.ram.

45 The Muslim Brother, Muhammad al-Majdhub, recounts that, the day Sayyid Qutb was sentenced to death, Ibn Baz asked him to write a telegram of protest to be sent to the Nasser regime. Al-Majdhub, shocked by the announcement of Qutb's imminent death, wrote the telegram using a totally uncompromising style. When he read it to Ibn Baz, convinced that the latter would ask him to moderate his language, he was surprised to see the blind shaykh approve of every word the telegram contained and ask for it to be sent immediately. This telegram was—according to al-Majdhub— the only such act of protest originating from the Muslim world that Nasser received on the occasion, see al-Majdhub, *'Ulama' wa mufakkirun 'araftuhum*, 91.

46 See al-Albani's tape entitled "Mafahim yajib 'an tusahhah" [Conceptions that need to be corrected].

47 The recording is available at: http://www.albrhan.org/fetan/a18.ram.

48 See al-Albani's tape entitled "*Salah al-zahir wa-l-batin*" [External and internal piety], 1.

49 al-Majdhub, *'Ulama' wa mufakkirun 'araftuhum*, 302.

50 Ibid.

51 For this fatwa, see, for instance, Wiktorowicz, *Management of Islamic Activism*, 169n76.

52 Muqbil al-Wadi'i, *al-Makhraj min al-fitna* [How to overcome discord] (Sanaa: n.p., 1982), 90.

53 Ibid., 96.

54 "Ansar al-Sunna al-Muhammadiyya" [The proponents of the prophetic tradition], a pro-Wahhabi Egyptian association founded in Cairo in 1926.

55 Al-Wadi'i, *al-Makhraj min al-fitna*, 99–100.

56 Ibid., 101–2.

57 Ibid., 106–14.

58 Ibid., 123.

59 Al-Albani, "Mafahim yajib 'an tusahhah."

60 The recording can be found at: http://www.islamgold.com/rmdata/139_Albani_qotob_part3.rm

61 Interview with former JSM member Nasir al-Huzaymi, Riyadh, March 2005.

62 Interview with a former member of the neo-Ahl al-Hadith, Jedda, April 2005.

63 Ibid.

64 *Annual Index of the Islamic University of Medina*, 1978, 209–10.

65 al-Majdhub, *'Ulama' wa mufakkirun 'araftuhum*, 151–75.

66 *Annual Index*, 209.

67 Ibid., 113.

68 Ibid., 225.

69 Reinhard Schulze, *Islamischer Internationalismus im 20. Jahrhundert* (Leiden: Brill, 1990), 142.

70 As elaborated in Chapter 1.

71 This presentation of the Jamis is the result of field observation and interviews conducted in Saudi Arabia between 2003 and 2006.

72 Wiktorowicz, *Management of Islamic Activism*, 110–46.

73 Samir Amghar, "Les Salafistes français: une nouvelle aristocratie religieuse?," *Maghreb-Machrek* 183 (Spring 2005), 15.